Mem

Miracle

A Journey; from Destitution to Deliverance

_____

John D. McHugh Jr.

11/12/2018

Dear ~~████████~~

It has been a pleasure to meet you. Hope you enjoy my story. Feel free to pass it along to whoever needs a hand

All the Best

John

Dedication

I wrote this book to honor my friends who didn't survive, those who still struggle, and their families and friends. I wanted to present the humanity, charity, and kindness shown me by those who had nothing. I want their mothers and fathers to know their children mattered; they helped me in times of need, shared their food or booze, or gave me a blanket on a cold night. Without their assistance I would have perished years ago.

In the memory of those whose lives guided me, although they could never find their own way: Gregory Anton Duff, Samuel Perry Clarke, Peter Scott Cummings, Bob Pardini, Tommy Muldoone, David Sterling, Milano John, Terry Crumb, Dave Bernie, Murphy, Bernadine, Sheryl, Jack, Ritchie and Sugar the Dog, Catfish, Marvin, Fabio, Joanne, Ron from Maple, Billy Clarke, Kelly Harper, the two Bills and the countless others I met along the way.

Foreword

I never did anything half-assed, including destroying my own life.

It's hard to tell where my story begins or ends. Even now I keep trying to figure it out. Every time I thought I had the starting point nailed down, another memory crept in. When I was sure I knew the ending, life threw me a few more curveballs, and more outlandish anecdotes appeared.

In the end I decided to start in the middle and see how far I could inch out on the branch before it tore free from the trunk and I tumbled to the ground.

-John

They peer from beneath darkened, dank overpasses cordoned off with cardboard, fabric, and trash. They rattle past bedroom windows in the dead of night, dragging shopping carts filled with all their earthly possessions. They collapse during daylight hours to sleep on park benches or in church pews, exhausted from surviving yet another night. The dawn of a new day simply means the whole process must begin again.

There is no real hope, only the slim chance that tomorrow may be different, maybe just a little better. They cling to that notion like a drowning man clutches a rope.

The Hunger and Homelessness Survey, released by the US Conference of Mayors in 2012, found that on a single freezing night in January, 633,782 people slept in the street. Not counting people in cities outside the survey, or those who hide from the survey takers, those driven underground by fear and shame.

Many of these transients are the drunks and dope fiends who comprise a third of the homeless population. Others have never recovered from losing jobs or family. Some are unable to deal with mental illness or are fleeing domestic violence; a great many of these are children. Only 6% of homeless people are living so voluntarily. On any given day, the homeless are nine times more likely to die than the general population.

The life expectancy of a homeless person is thirty years shorter for men (age 47) and thirty-five years shorter for women (age 43).

The outlook is bleak. Recovery from "chronic" homelessness, those unfortunate enough to be on the streets for more than a year, is practically nonexistent, but once in a very great while a miracle occurs. The following is an account of one of those miracles.

5

UCSF Medical Center November 2, 2005

I dread the night.

The darkened hours that reduce me to a trembling mass of equal parts worry and regret. Agonizing over the things I should have done, fretting over the obstacles I have yet to face. For me now it is different, it doesn't matter anymore. I am doomed, and I know it.

The omniscient ones in the blue scrubs and starched white coats summed it all up quite succinctly, in their detached, robotic tone. "Your heart is functioning at 7% of normal, We have never seen anyone survive at less than ten."

I lay in the cool, antiseptic air of the hospital room, the temperature always kept low to limit the spread of bacteria. Shivering more from my current state of affairs than from the cold, a blinding flash of light burst through the swinging door as the night nurse pushed his cart to my bedside.

"Oh, you're awake," he said. "Right arm or left? It's up to you."

I raised both arms slowly from the mattress struggling with the task that would have been effortless a week before.

"It doesn't matter," I replied, studying the purple discolorations now covering my once perfectly bronzed skin. "Just use the side you're on."

He looked first at my left arm, then the right. Searching my forearms for a fresh clear spot between the bruises.

"Yeah you're pretty beat up; let's go with the right," he decided.

Stretching the skin taut between his thumb and forefinger, the RN poked the needle through and drew a little more life out through the syringe.

"That should do it."

As if anything they were doing now still mattered. He was drawing blood from a corpse, and for the life of me, I couldn't understand why.

This was not some righteous struggle against a rare and aggressive cancer. I was not the innocent victim of a tragic accident clinging to life. I was not even a man whose high stress job, fatty diet, and refusal to exercise had conspired to explode his heart. I was just a parasite. A burden. A bum. I was a drunk

I wanted to blame my afflictions on a multitude of tough breaks. Sadly, all the bad luck and misfortune was not due to chance. It was forged rock solid by my own hands.

I had been told for years to stop, but I refused to listen. Now, it was hopeless. My life was a wreck. My heart was failing, and in short, I had gotten what I deserved.

In the past I would have left the hospital despite the doctor's strenuous objections. Either legitimately by signing out against medical advice or by dressing silently in the blackness and slipping away down a back stairway.

This time it was different. I lacked both the strength and fortitude needed to mount an escape attempt. The bed was safe, comfortable, warm, and dry. What lay outside the hospital walls was anybody's guess. My battered body teetered on the brink of catastrophic failure.

So, I pulled the covers tight to my neck and turned slowly onto my left side. The IVs tugged at the crook of my arm, the weight of the fluid within them pulling against the tape and needle holding them in place.

Things had not always been this way, never this bad. In fact my life, now painfully abbreviated, had been quite enjoyable even as I relinquished more and more control to the booze.

Carefree days spent with friends, wiling away the hours in a state of alcohol induced euphoria while some relentless, invisible accountant kept track of the costs.

Now the bill, long past due, would have to be paid. I lay in the blackness watching the electrocardiograph monitor my vital signs. I wondered would I cling to life long enough to see my heart rate read zero? Or would I lose consciousness before the flat line buzzer sounded? Either way, it was only a matter of time.

The minutes ticked by. Would I make it until the sun rose again? Or was every passing second moving me closer to a barren, solitary end?

Funny thing, but even as I despised what I had become, I fondly recalled every minute that got me here.

A smile crept across my face accompanied by some painful but much needed laughter.

"Lose the drama, John," I moaned into the silence. "You know you had the time of your life."

Golden Gate Park, San Francisco, 2005

A bright flash of lightning lit up the morning sky followed shortly by a loud low rumble. The alarm clock had sounded.

"God my life sucks!" I shouted into the cold damp February morning.

A plea, a prayer or perhaps just an accurate assessment of my life, even today it is hard to say. An unsolicited response of "Mine too," followed by a chorus of anonymous giggles drifted through the fog and mist forcing me to smile.

The night, like a hundred before, had been spent sleeping, or attempting to, in the northeast corner of Golden Gate Park just off Stanyan Street. I pushed back the blue nylon tarp and wriggled free of my waterlogged sleeping bag. I too was drenched; my clothes clung to my shivering body sagging from the water's weight. Stuffing my wet feet into even wetter socks and boots, I squished to a standing position. My head swam as the breath puffed from my mouth like a struggling steam engine traversing a long uphill grade. I stumbled forward scanning the scrub brush for the 40 ounce Steele 211 malt liquor I had stashed the night before. Years of experience had taught me well the need for a morning wakeup. Far too many days this past year had begun with my hands shaking from the DT's, my stomach knotted with the dry heaves, fearing a seizure as every cell in my body screamed out for booze.

The "cure" was never far from where I laid down the night before. I soon found the bottle beneath a pile of wet leaves, its label peeling from the glass as I greedily snatched it up. I stretched my sleeve over my hand to wipe the dirt from the neck. Spinning off the top in one fluid

9

motion, I guzzled down close to a third of the bottle, my Adam's Apple bobbing up and down as the heady liquid filled my empty gut. Good and cold just the way I liked it, thanks to the harsh weather.

My plan of attack the night before had been simple enough. The forecasters unanimously called for heavy rains. I constructed a lean-to with my tarp tucked along the hillside above the horseshoe Pits, a stand of pine trees providing cover from the rear. Hiding me away from the prying eyes of the rangers and police who patrolled even the smallest trails, scouring the park in search of vagrants like me. These bastions of law enforcement seemed to take particular delight in rousting the park populace who flocked to the tunnels and doorways for shelter when the weather turned nasty. I steered clear of these spots knowing they offered little more than a ride in the paddy wagon down to 850 Bryant, the San Francisco County Jail.

The rain came as promised but with the tarp above me and my ground cover nestled in the dry porous sand I figured to be fine until morning. I scratched a shallow trench along the sides of my shelter to accommodate the runoff from the hill and tarp. I spread out the sleeping bag, slid my few belongings into a black plastic trash bag, tucking the sack into my backpack to act as a pillow at the head of my bed.

My small transistor radio, purchased from Goodwill a fortnight before, tuned to NPR, filled the night with a sizzling debate on the pros and cons of a flat tax rate. Leaning back I contentedly nursed a large bottle of a tasty, unpretentious Merlot, a vintage I had never sampled before or since. Each swig was sweet on my tongue, warming my being as well as my belly.

I had pulled off my purchase of the wine and my "cure" by bartering three twelve packs of Thomas' English muffins given to me at a church lunch, along with three dollars cash.

"Wow," the kindly, rotund woman at the church lunch commented, "You must really like English muffins."

"Well," I replied honestly, "they are not all for me."

In truth none of them were for me. I was well known at the local stores, where they would be traded and resold to supply me with what I really wanted. My chicanery had secured the needed alcohol leaving me still solvent with $6.39 for the coming day, overall, not too bad. I had been in far worse shape over the years.

I stood to relieve myself before slipping into the warmth of the bag, vino clutched tightly to my chest; I drifted into a deep satisfying slumber. All was well until I awoke around 3 a.m. to again answer Mother Nature's call. The tarp was now just inches above my face, swollen like a pregnant sow with thirty gallons of accumulated rainwater, the rain continued to fall in buckets, driven by what I approximated to be gale force winds. I used some branches to create a crib to support the tarp. My sleep no longer deep and sound, I waited for the storm to subside, hoping my makeshift repair would spare me the agony of being swept away in a flash flood. Throwing caution to the wind I drank the last of the wine and said a quick prayer to Saint Jude, patron of desperate cases and lost causes.

Saint Jude must have dozed off shortly after I did. The tarp broke loose, releasing a cascade of freezing water. The ensuing deluge caused me to pee both my pants and sleeping bag. Now lying in three inches of water, unable to extricate myself from the saturated mummy bag I shrunk into the fetal position and waited for the cardiac arrest sure to follow in the wake of the icy torrent, hoping its arrival would free me from both my misery and self-disgust.

Fate was not so kind. The storm raged on and I resigned myself to wait for the cawwing of the large crows announcing the break of day. No longer did I get up to pee, opting instead to savor any warmth the good Lord might permit me on this hellish night. The lightning flashed, the thunder roared and finally I survived to face another day.

The 8.1% alcohol content of the Steele Reserve began to work its magic, seeping into every corner of my brain to rejuvenate the pleasant buzz from the night before. As always this building euphoria filled me with a new sense of optimism and purpose.

My first task was to get rid of the rancid clothing I wore. My backpack contained the needed dry clothes. Not much but it was a start. I made my way out to Stanyan Street and the back entrance to Saint Mary's Hospital.

Moving quickly through the gleaming glass and chrome doors along Hayes Street, I entered the complex. It was still very early and the bulk of the workforce had not yet arrived. The emptiness made my task much easier as any employee would have taken one look at me and called security. I didn't see a soul as I stealthily navigated the corridors to a small restroom tucked away in the surgical area's waiting room, the perfect spot for my metamorphosis.

Surgery didn't begin at the hospital 'til about 8 a.m. and most people waited in the main lobby. Best of all, the restroom door locked giving me the ten or fifteen minutes of privacy I needed to complete my transformation. I stripped down, scrubbed, shampooed and shaved. Donning clean, respectable clothes topped with a Haight Street Fair hoodie to keep me warm, and my trademark Ray Bans to keep me cool. The soiled rags I'd worn went straight into the trash. I cleaned the sink and floor to avoid

12

any problems with the security staff. When you live in the woods burning bridges is not an option. I exited the building by a different route, nodding a polite good morning to the workers heading in to start their day. The only trace of the harrowing night the squeak of my still wet boots on the gleaming tile of the hospital floor.

Returning to camp I packed the wet sleeping gear in the plastic trash bag, crammed everything into my backpack and shouldered the load. My high tech sleeping bag weighed barely five pounds dry; this morning it was closer to fifty. The night was past, I was essentially warm and dry, and the first rays of the sun pierced the famous San Francisco fog.

I knew a shelter downtown where I could do a load of laundry for fifty cents. Travel and washing, however, would take the better part of the day and my funds were extremely limited. I stopped at Cala Foods on the corner of Haight and Stanyan to replenish my meager reserve. Crossing the parking lot I heard the familiar baritone of Earl, the security guard.

"Hey Johnny, what's up?" the graying black man said with a wave.

"Not much man, just heading downtown to do some laundry after last night."

"You outside last night?" Earl asked in disbelief.

"Yeah, all night long." I replied.

"You look pretty good for all that."

"I have my ways, my friend."

"I bet you do Johnny, I bet you do," Earl said.

I had become friendly with Earl about four months earlier when he asked if I could loan him a dollar for coffee before he began his shift. I handed him four quarters, surprised that a man with a real job was putting the touch on me. When he reached for the change I could see telltale burns on his fingertips. Raising my gaze to his face I saw more burns barely visible on his lips. Earl had been smoking some kind of dope the night before -- probably crack or speed -- I didn't bother to ask which one.

"Having some fun last night?"

A conspiratorial smirk crossed his face. I nodded back, his secret safe with me. Since Cala and McDonalds comprised the hub at the entrance to the park, Earl and I crossed paths nearly every day.

At one point he said to me, "Johnny you got to boost something don't worry about me, I ain't gonna be chasing you down the street."

"Thanks Earl but I don't steal."

"Really?" he asked. As if all vagrants must also be thieves.

"Just not my style," I replied.

"Well I'll be," said Earl with a shake of his head.

I left him that day pleased at the carte blanche he offered, my reward for friendship and silence.

Stopping just outside the automatic doors I dug into my pack's outside pocket to find the Ziploc bag that kept my food stamps safe and dry. I had $78 left from the $129 I received each month from the Federal government.

The stamps, to my mind, were not charity; since I would never reach retirement age they were a small dividend due me on the taxes and Social Security paid over the twenty five years I had worked prior to my departure from mainstream America. I went to the produce section and picked out ten cherry tomatoes. I headed for the register and paid for them one at a time with a $1 food stamp, receiving the change in cash. This maneuver irritated the clerk but netted me 75 or 80¢ per tomato, doubling the cash in my pocket. I would hustle up more along the way. It was just after nine and my morning buzz was beginning to fade. I made my way up Haight Street munching cherry tomatoes to Haight and Cole Liquors, or as it is known to the locals, "Fuck You Frank's."

Frank stood at his post behind the register, the wood floor worn into a shiny hollow beneath his feet. He had been in the same spot every day for as long as anyone could remember, at least thirty years.

"Mornin' Frank," I said with a short wave.

"Hello. Fuck You," the portly Middle Easterner replied.

I walked to the rear cooler and opened the door. The cloud from my breath lingered in the still, icy air. I selected two more Steel 211's and returned to the register to pay. Frank resumed his taunting, a ritual I would surely miss when he or I was gone.

"You're very nice, nice looking too. Are you gay?"

"Yes, but don't tell anyone."

"No, I tell everyone," he roared. "I make some money on you!"

"You already make too much money on me," I told him.

"Yeah, I guess so," he replied.

"You know so," I added.

I handed him a five and he juggled the two quarters due me, flipping them from his palm to the back of his hairy hand. Finally he launched the change high in the air above the red Marlboro display that housed the shop's cigarettes. I snatched the quarters from the air.

"Nice catch," he barked, obviously disappointed that I wasn't chasing the money all over the floor.

I slid the beer into my backpack and barked my last "Fuck You!"

Frank waved me towards the door, "Fuck you too, and have a nice day."

With my supplies restocked it was time to head downtown. I turned south along Cole Street and ran straight into a trio of my fellow derelicts -- Marvin, Mark and Catfish -- panhandling to purchase their own supply of booze. I gave one of them the two quarters, grateful that I had slipped my liquor into the pack. Had I emerged from the store with the bottles clanking together in a plastic bag I would have had my own parade of bums, an alcoholic entourage nipping at my heels until both were drained dry. The boys headed to Frank's to purchase beer and exchange pleasantries. I beat it up the hill towards the N-Judah train, the light rail that ran the length of San Francisco from Ocean Beach to the Bay Bridge.

"John McHugh, my worst nightmare, as I live and breathe."

Her voice boomed, unmistakable in this quiet, bohemian neighborhood. Rounding the corner in an ankle length black leather coat and matching boots was Tanya

Rains, my confidante, co-conspirator and most of all, friend.

Tanya was regarded as a local celebrity or a public nuisance depending on whom you spoke to and whether or not they carried a badge. Her changing hair color, indicative of her diverse moods, ran the gamut from subdued, mousy brown to outrageous, no holds barred, suicide blonde. I was pleased to see today she sported a stylish, shiny black Asian style coif. Her bangs hung straight at her eyebrows, a loose curl arched into her neck just above the shoulder. Tanya's gorgeous steel blue eyes only added to the incongruity. She would surely be the front-runner in a "Girl Most Likely to Get Away with Murder" contest, an imaginative maniac who inspired me to new levels of insanity and mayhem. I had not seen her for at least a week and delighted in her reappearance.

"What have you been up to?" I queried with genuine interest.

"Not too much, just writing a new book." She flirted, batting her eyes.

"What's it about?"

"A kid's book called, "There's a Mouse in My House," she said digging in her bag, eventually producing a small notebook.

"This is it. What do you think?" she said, handing me the book.

I thumbed through the pages of short verses and funky illustrations.

"I think it's great. How about a drink?"

"Twist my arm," she replied.

"Let's get off Front Street then. How about up by the train?" I said.

"Lead the way."

We walked to the train stop and sat on a bench tucked between two bushes. Good cover in a place where people normally sit and wait equals an ideal drinking spot.

"What's in the bag?" she asked

"Everything I own, all my earthly possessions," I answered.

I recounted the events of the night before as we swigged the beer and caught up on the latest Haight Street gossip. I could feel the booze start to take effect and feared I would fail in my quest to wash and dry my sleeping gear. Tanya had spent the night inside with one of the many friends she had in the Haight so she was far from sympathetic with my need to get the job done. The weather was clearing but I wanted to avoid another miserable night sleeping in soaking wet gear. I managed to wrangle an agreement from her that we could do anything she wanted as long as I got the laundry done. We knocked off the last of the first bottle and left the bench staying well toward the rear of the train to time our jump.

The N-Judah train is part of the San Francisco MUNI system. A two-car light rail trolley that ran above ground from Ocean Beach into downtown San Francisco, becoming a subway at Church Street where it ran the length of Market Street. The beauty of the N-Judah was that when the train stopped all the doors opened to allow riders to exit. This allowed bums like us to enter without paying the fare at the front door. Most of the passengers had monthly passes or transfers that meant they could enter through any door.

Ticket checks were sporadic at best and if we got a summons, a trip to the Homeless Coalition would squash the ticket, so the system proved an easy mark for those unable or unwilling to pay.

The train crested the hill its trailing wire sparking as it scraped the overhead power cable. A quick inspection as it rolled past showed no ticket checkers inside. The doors opened and we stole aboard, plopping contentedly into the molded plastic bench seat.

"Open the other beer," Tanya said.

"Not on the train, T. Let's wait until we get off." It wasn't the fear of getting a ticket or being dragged off to jail that prevented me from popping the top, it was the loss of the beer itself. Going to jail had long ago ceased to bother me but the thought of some smug condescending MUNI cop pouring out my precious juice was enough to make me toe the line and not drink on the train. Had I been a little more intoxicated no consequence would have been great enough to deter me.

Tanya twisted her face in a screwy perplexed fashion and said, "We need a cup, a big one."

"Why, are we going to beg?" I asked.

"You said you have money."

"Relax, I do. So why would we need a cup?"

She slowly looked left, then right, scanning the train for prying eyes. "Camouflage," she whispered.

"Oh, I get it. I'll get one when we stop."

We left the train at Montgomery Street, opened the second beer and the search for a cup began. Along Market, then Mission, we would embrace in doorways, looking for the police over each other's shoulder before stealing a few sips.

When the beer was gone we stopped at a bodega on Fourth Street under the freeway to buy more.

"Don't forget the cup," she added as I walked to the door.

"It's kind of nice without the cup," I noted.

"Sure is." She smiled and gave me a hug, adding "I miss these muscles."

"I missed you too and I won't forget the cup."

The 32-ounce foam cold cup, complete with a lid and straw set us back another quarter but it was perfect camouflage for its contents. We ducked into the alley next to the shop; I kept watch while she filled the cup to the brim. Carefully, she let the beer run down the side so it didn't foam up.

"Perfect Johnny Boy," she beamed with pride.

We walked the last block to the shelter to wash my things. Luck was with us, the break in the weather had allowed people to go outside; the place was fairly empty which made the task that much quicker and easier. I started the machine as we sipped the beer from our covert cup.

"We need some more cash," I announced.

"Are we out?" she asked.

"Almost, I've got two bucks and some change but also about seventy in stamps."

"That'll work. Guess we're going to see Mamasan," she said.

"Yes dear, as soon as we're done."

Mamasan was the generic name for any of a few dozen Asian women who paid cash for food stamps. They could be found on corners in the Tenderloin or any other low-income neighborhood. Typically they paid sixty cents on the dollar but if you bartered well you might get seventy-five.

While the sleeping bag swirled round and round in the warm air of the humming dryer we killed the cup and headed outside to fill it with the last of our hooch. I shook out the tarp, rolling it tightly and lashing it to the pack while Tanya took care of the refill.

Twenty minutes later I did the same with the bag and we headed across Market Street to the Tenderloin.

A new day was dawning, the clouds and fog were gone, the buzz from the beer exhilarating and Tanya walked alongside me, six or seven hours had turned my life around. That's how life seemed to go on the streets -- all or nothing -- you just had to make sure that the nothings didn't kill you.

A Mamasan was easy to spot. It was a wonder that they weren't all arrested but they performed a valuable, albeit illegal, service so I guess the police just couldn't be bothered. They all wore large floppy straw hats that shielded them from the sun and size 3 Nikes. I spied one standing in a thrift store doorway. Tanya waited on the corner while I brokered the deal.

21

"Hello Mama, I've got some stamps, $50.00. How much?"

"Twenty-five" she snapped.

"No, no, I need thirty-five."

"Thirty, no more, you go"

"OK, thirty."

We walked behind a white municipal van parked at the curb. By the time we cleared the far side the deal was done. I returned to Tanya, Mamasan to her thrift store doorway.

"How'd you do?" she asked.

"Thirty for fifty," I replied. "Saved a $20 stamp for food."

"Well done, John," she said smiling.

"Where to?" I asked.

"I'm the boss?" she asked.

"That was the deal and besides, you're always the boss."

"Don't you forget it, mister."

We began the trek up Market Street to Church where the N-Judah exited the tunnel. A Safeway supermarket along the way would outfit us for dinner.

"Can we go by the ducks?" Tanya asked.

"Sure, the barbeques are right there and I know you love the ducks," I answered.

"Haven't seen them in quite a while," she mused more to herself than me.

"I am sure they've missed you too."

As we arrived at Safeway I asked, "Who's doing the cooking?"

"You do dinner, I'll do breakfast," she replied.

"Staying the night?" I asked hopefully.

"Well, we can share a blanket, can't we?"

That meant sleeping together for warmth, safety and security, but no sex.

"We'll see how that goes," I said.

"Yes, we will," she answered neither confirming nor denying.

A nice steak, potatoes, vegetables and the supplies for Tanya's breakfast came to $21.78. I dropped the remaining $20 stamp on the counter. Tanya reeled in mock horror as I paid the balance in cash. Food was easy to come by in San Francisco as dozens of churches and shelters served up meals for the destitute. Hard currency was reserved for one's drug of choice, in our case, alcohol. I pulled her tight by the waist and kissed her.

"We'll survive," I whispered as our lips parted.

"We always do," she added.

We caught the first N-Judah train, climbing aboard through the rear door as usual, two drifters heading west into the setting sun. Tanya let out a little yawn with a squeal at the end.

"Excuse me," she said. "I'm tired."

"Yep," I replied.

"And hungry."

I patted the Safeway bag.

"Thirsty too."

"We can stop at Danny's. He had wine on sale last week, a big bottle for five bucks." I said.

Charlie's Market was another of the incongruities that made San Francisco so attractive to those who like their town to be just a little off key. It was owned by Danny, operated by Danny and called Danny's by everyone in the neighborhood yet a huge porcelain sign stood in the parking lot proclaiming it to actually be Charlie's Market. No one, including Danny, knew of anyone named Charlie remotely connected with the place yet still its official name was Charlie's. Go figure.

We left the train and entered the market to pick up the wine. I found a half-gallon of robust port sure to go nicely with the meat for the bargain price of five dollars. Danny's daughter, a pretty Middle Eastern girl, stood behind the register.

"How about some brandy too?" Tanya asked as politely as she could. I answered with a scowl.

"Well, it might get cold," she added.

"A pint of E&J also please."

The total was just over the ten-dollar bill I set on the counter. I dug into my empty pockets with a sheepish expression.

"Don't worry about it," the young lady said.

"Thank you very much and have a great night."

"You too," she added with a smile.

Before we had even reached the curb Tanya spoke. "Are we broke again?"

I was tempted to say something about not needing the brandy but things were going so well I just paused a second to gather my thoughts and told her the truth. "We need the twenty for tomorrow, I wasn't breaking it for nine cents."

"Johnny, you sneaky dog," she said with a smile. Tanya's version of a compliment.

The Duck Pond, officially named South Lake, sat a block away in the southwest corner of Golden Gate Park. We arrived at the picnic area as the sun dipped into the Pacific just ten blocks west.

A kaleidoscope of fiery red, deep purple and maroon mixed with the yellow sun to create a sunset rarely seen outside a travel brochure.

Tanya sat at the table unpacking the food, as I hunted up the makings of our fire. Pulling half of a San Francisco Chronicle from a trashcan I added some twigs and lit the fire. One of the best fuels that doesn't require felling a tree are pinecones. I piled a half dozen on the burning sticks and soon had a nice bed of coals and rolling flame.

The corn went husk and all into the pond to soak. I stuck the potatoes with my Buck knife and laid them to bake on the grill above the coals. I realized that I was still wearing my pack with the bedrolls. Living outside meant you never put anything important down because it would disappear in a blink and you would be left to start all over again. I walked to the table, stowed my backpack beneath it and sat next to Tanya who stared vacantly at the fire's hypnotic glow.

"How long John, I'm getting hungry," she asked.

"Half an hour. I'll put the steak and corn on for the last fifteen minutes."

We were both mesmerized by the flames twisting, spiraling in the dark night.

"Hey, John."

"Yeah, T."

"We can't open the wine, we need a corkscrew."

"There's one on my knife," I said, handing her the Buck.

"I thought we had to push it in with a stick."

"Not tonight, sweetie."

She opened the wine and I opened the brandy. We filled the deep cap full of E&J, each taking a shot.

"Go easy on that," she cautioned. "I need you awake tonight."

"Why, whatever for?" I asked, feigning innocence.

"To guard my precious ass," she answered.

"I'll guard it, kiss it, bite it..."

She cut me short, "Promises, promises."

I pulled the corn from the pond and placed it whole on the coals. The potatoes were nearly done so I dropped the steak beside them on the grill. Flames leapt into the air. I felt a rush, a satisfaction, driven by a primal urge present since Paleolithic man first applied fire to flesh.

"What happened to the wine?" I asked.

Tanya pulled the bottle from its confines beneath the table. I reached for it but she pushed my hand away.

"You drink too fast," she scolded me.

"I bought it," I reminded her.

"True, true." She scrunched her face again looking left and right, pondering a solution.

"Come here," she ordered.

Grabbing my face she pinched my cheeks together. I puckered like a blowfish and she poured a portion of wine into my mouth.

"Much better," she pronounced pulling me to her and planting a kiss on my still puckered lips. I could not argue with her logic.

I tended the steak carefully between fish pucker sips of wine.

Tanya asked, "Any plates Johnny boy?"

I rinsed the steak's foam tray with water, wiped it clean, then piled it high with food.

The steak was medium well, charred black on the outside with just the right amount of juice dripping from its faint pink center, the corn puffy and moist roasted in its husk, the potatoes baked to perfection. We had to share the knife but I had a few sporks, along with a pile of napkins from Taco Bell.

"This is really good," she said. "You can cook."

"I should have gotten a candle," I said dreamily. "You know, I was thinking more about eating than romance but I guess they go hand in hand."

"Sounds nice, maybe tomorrow."

I was very pleased, sated by the food, warmed by the wine, and above all hopeful; it was rare I could mention Tanya and tomorrow in the same breath.

We cleaned up and packed away all the gear and food.

"Johnny, I need a bathroom. Any ideas?"

"Sure, there's one up the hill by the Polo Field."

"It'll be locked."

"No problem, I have a key."

We wove through the woods along the bike trail that led up the hill to the Polo Fields. It would have been quicker to go straight up Middle Drive but after dark, especially carrying sleeping bags in the park, it was unwise to use any route accessible by car. Along with the fields atop the hill sits the Golden Gate Park Stables and Police Station. In an effort to avoid contact with the cops we stayed south of everything until the bathrooms came in sight. As expected the bathroom was locked I fished the key from my pack and opened the door locking it again once we were inside. Tanya went to a stall and I flipped over a large steel trash pail climbing on top of it to keep watch outside the high barred window. The lights remained on all night to discourage vandals and the last thing I needed was a trespassing charge.

"Where'd you get the key?" Tanya asked her forceful voice echoing off the tile walls.

"Sshhhh!" I whispered "Clarence the ranger gave it to me works on all the bathroom locks, handy huh?"

"Very, let me get some mountain money and let's get out of here."

The Mountain Money reference park slang for toilet paper made me chuckle again.

"OK, ready," I said, "let's go."

We swung out the door locking it behind us, moved quickly to the tree line and the cover of darkness retracing our steps back towards the duck pond. I swung the half empty bottle of wine by the neck while Tanya played with the radio changing stations incessantly as was her custom. Had I given her a diamond ring or trip to Hawaii I doubt she would have been any happier.

We crossed the park by way of the golf course stopping at the forth tee to down another shot of E&J. Now it really was getting cold.

I loved my buzz tonight, loved everything about it. The combination of beer and wine fortified with a couple shots of brandy rounded the edges of my vision, wrapping my mind in a blanket of euphoria. Being here in the night with Tanya made it that much better, but I could have been with all by myself as long as there was booze. During the hundreds of AA meetings I had attended, at any of the dozen or so rehabs I had tried I was told my drinking was but a symptom of my illness.

I begged to differ; I was intelligent and hardworking when I chose to be. I did not suffer from any mental or physical illness. I was not abused or mistreated as a child. In fact due to my own choices I had become the black sheep of a loving family who would have given anything to help me. All of my wounds were self-inflicted, my scars forged by my own hands.

I had decided about five years before that the only thing I really liked to do was drink. The booze obliterated all that

29

was bad in my life, intensified all that was good. I moved from New York to California kidding myself that I was being noble by removing the burden of me from my family and friends. When in fact the reason I left was to be able to drink with impunity. To drink without anyone telling me to stop. Without anyone pointing out how much I was hurting them or how self-destructive my behavior was. I had been wallowing in this mindset for nearly a decade, but here on this night the heavens had aligned.

This was the reason I drank to feel just like this, to achieve the perfect buzz.

"Johnny, where are we heading?" Tanya casually asked.

"I found a spot on the far side of the golf course no one's seen it but me, never showed it to anyone."

"Is it safe?" she asked.

"You'll soon see." I answered.

The area was prime camping territory with the golf course along one side, North Lake along the other and no houses near. There were no flowers nearby for the gardeners to tend. The maintenance yard was clear on the other side of the park. A single small trail snaked beside a huge growth of thorn bushes. Rising majestically from the center was a stand of monstrous pines.

I had found the site about a month before while returning from the beach. From the outside the scraggly thorns looked impregnable my curiosity had determined they were not.

"Take hold of the pack Tanya and watch your eyes." I told her, weaving my way along the thin serpentine game trail twisting between the thorns.

30

"Where are you taking me?" she demanded.

"Just a little more..."

We popped free of the thorns under the branches of the pines. The trees had grown so tall with the thorns shading the bottom that the lowest branches were six or seven feet off the ground.

"Wow," Tanya exclaimed in wonder "it's like a cave."

"Hold on, there's more."

I pointed to what appeared to be a rock tucked in the corner to the left. I walked to its base and lifted the edge.

"A tarp?" asked Tanya.

"Yep, a brown one, add a few branches and instant boulder, hides everything."

"What, pray tell is everything?" she inquired.

I rolled back the tarp to reveal my treasure trove of survival gear. A flashlight, extra clothes, some toiletries and a trash bag full of blankets garnered from church handouts and finds on the beach. I had several smaller items batteries, a p38 can opener, some cutlery, dishes and pots things taken for granted in a normal home proved priceless living outdoors.

As my morning had clearly illustrated our biggest adversary was the weather. We had others like; the police charged with getting rid of the hundreds of homeless who lived in the park or the park workers who would pack up any gear they stumbled upon, but the worst by far was rain. A top the pile sat my best defense.

"Even a tent?" asked Tanya.

"Yes, I bought it from Keys" an old train jumper we both knew, "for twenty five bucks, pretty close to brand new."

"Guess you thought of everything."

"Lord Knows I've tried." I mumbled

I cleared an area of sticks and rocks and began layering the blankets one atop the other. Afterwards I unzipped the sleeping bag and topped off the bed. Tanya propped the wine and radio at the head of our hobo's bed. Taking off her jacket she plopped down to remove her shoes.

We opened the brandy and shared a few sips before putting it down for the night. Snuggled tight in the warmth of the sleeping bag.

Tanya whispered in my ear, "Johnny boy, Momma needs some lovin'."

"Well come here then," I replied.

Later, we lay in each other's arms beneath a canopy of stars intermittently visible between the swaying pine boughs. Tanya's breathing became soft, relaxed. She slept deeply not quite snoring more purring like a kitten. I lay at her side recounting the events, or rather, the turn of events of this magical day. The smell of our sweat mingled with the faint aroma of her perfume and the woodsy scent of pine.

Hours earlier, I had barely been able to crawl to my feet. Now I lay safe and warm, a beautiful woman in my arms, without a care in the world. I did not have to get up early the next morning; rent, bills, a job, were not even on my radar.

People often look at the homeless with a mix of pity and disdain.

"Look at that bum, how could they have let themselves get like that?"

They see only the end result of years of not caring. On Day One you still care about everything. Within a year bad decisions have colluded with unseen circumstances and all you care about is getting to the next day. But there are many days and nights like the one Tanya and I just shared. Each serves to reinforce the obsession that on any given day things will turn around. The mind filters out the hundreds of horrors and dwells only on those shining moments. That is how we survive.

Tonight I was doing better than surviving. I pulled Tanya tight and thanked God for an exceptional day. The tranquility of the night coupled with the contentment inherent in the day's successes overwhelmed me and I slept deep, silent, sound.

* * *

The cars moved fast along Fulton, at least fifteen miles above the posted limit. Workers on their way from the Great Highway into downtown San Francisco, rousting me from the best sleep I'd had in months. I tried to slide my arm from beneath Tanya's head. She elbowed me soundly in the ribs.

"Go back to sleep!" she barked.

She lifted her head. I pulled my arm free. Tanya fluffed the blanket and slammed her head down on it, pulling the sleeping bag up to hide from the brilliant morning. I stood stark naked and peed off into the thorn bushes, relishing in the freedom of this decadent act. Turning back I surveyed the campsite, clothes strewn everywhere along the ground, the empty wine bottle propped at the head of our hobo bed, like the morning after an outrageous frat party. I peeked out at the surroundings trying to see the hilltop beyond the thorns. I could not make it out. We were safe. If I couldn't see out, then no one could see in. I was thankful for that.

Fumbling through the wreckage, fallout from our passion the night before, I found my clothes and dressed. I checked my wallet for the twenty and found it nestled safely between the soft leather folds. I sat on an old stump pulling on one sock as I scanned the pile of blankets for the other.

Tanya began to stir and the sock magically appeared as she sat and drew the blanket up to cover her breasts. Her hair stuck out in all directions, her face puffy from sleep, her ankles and feet still covered in socks protruding from the covers like a Muppet sitting on a wall.

34

I wanted to tell her how adorable she looked but I knew better. I helped gather her clothes accompanied by a chorus of,

"Dammit! Shit! Damn you, John! You Ass!" until she finally sputtered her first coherent thought of the day. "I need Coffee."

"I'll go get you some if you're okay alone."

"Go. I'll be fine," she said pulling her pants up under the sleeping bag. "Where's the brandy?"

I pulled the brandy from the pack and took a short pull handing her the bottle. I coughed and nearly vomited.

"Too much for me," I gasped.

She sniffed the top and held it at arm's length.

"Me too. Go get coffee," she ordered.

"Are you sure you'll be all right?"

"Yes, yes now go."

Out of concern I handed her my knife, which she promptly threw at me.

"What no machine gun?" she roared. "Now go get my damn coffee!"

"I'll be back in twenty minutes," I hollered over my shoulder.

"You better be!" the thorns shouted back.

I crossed Fulton and headed up 43rd to Cabrillo and Joe's Market for Tanya's coffee and my morning wakeup. Joe or "Blockhead Joe" was a bit of an oddity, a tall, young Asian guy with a very large head. Like most names around here it passed along from one person to the next; no one knew who coined it but if it fit, it stuck.

Joe never gave credit and if you were three cents short on a ten dollar purchase "No Sale," but his beer was ice cold, he opened early and he was close so I took the good with the bad. Along with the coffee and two bottles I grabbed another twenty-four ounce can of Saint Ides which I greedily chugged on the walk back. It was always best to hedge your bet.

"Incoming!" I shouted on my way back through the thorns. As I reached the pines I saw Tanya radiant in the morning sun.

The change was truly remarkable, her hair combed, lipstick and makeup fastidiously applied with all the blankets folded and ready to be packed away.

I stifled a "Good girl" and opted for, "My, what a wonderful surprise!"

"See, I can be domestic," she said. "In fact I kinda like it."

"Well thank you," I replied and meant it.

"I want a cigarette," Tanya announced.

"I would have gotten a pack," I stammered.

"No, I want one but I'm not going to have one. I've been quitting."

"Well good for you."

"The funny thing is every time I try to quit people will hand me smokes without me even asking. When I don't care about stopping and I'm dying for a drag then no one will part with one no matter how hard I beg," she explained.

"One of the great mysteries of life." I added, "Blow in a little dog's face and he bites you, drive him in the car and he has to stick his head out the window."

"Something like that. Did you get sugar?"

"And creamers. It's in the bag."

I opened a forty as she fixed her coffee, eyeing me, then the brandy, back to me, then the brandy.

"Go ahead, you don't have to ask."

"I didn't," she snickered.

I watched as she dumped some coffee on the ground and added a healthy belt of the E&J, sealed the top and shook the cup. She folded out the tab and slowly sipped. Smacking her lips Tanya raised the cup to appraise it.

"Oh nice, very nice," she decreed.

"I'll stick with the beer."

I packed the blankets along with the rest of the gear, covering the mound with the dark brown tarp. I tied the sleeping bag and ground cloth to the backpack and lifted it to my shoulder.

"Why do you carry all that stuff?" Tanya asked.

"Because I never know where I'll end up and I don't feel like sleeping in the dirt." I answered.

"We'll come back tonight," she said with a peck on my cheek. "I like it here."

"Happy to have you!" I answered with a smile.

We ducked from the camp and wove our way along the golf course back to the duck pond.

"Hey, they're all out today!" Tanya said pointing at the two-dozen ducks paddling about the pond.

"Look, there are two herons too," I said.

I set to making a fire while Tanya diced the leftovers, setting them atop the grill and scrambling in a few eggs. The eggs stiffened and I got out two sporks.

"Out of the pan?" she asked.

"Yep, no plates this morning."

"Just like out on the ol' trail," she kidded.

"You're a regular Annie Oakley," I said between bites of the tasty omelet.

"No, Calamity Jane," she smirked.

"We need to take inventory, kid," I explained as I dumped the contents of my pockets on the table.

Tanya dug through her purse and added a handful of change.

"Twelve thirty-eight and a full forty, better than I thought," I commented.

"Still got some brandy," said Tanya shaking the bottle by the neck, a couple ounces swishing around in the bottom.

"I've been in worse shape."

"We have been in worse shape."

"I stand corrected," I apologized. "Let's see if I, no we, can get a tab. If we stock up on beer we should be good till tomorrow."

"Can you?" she asked.

"Can we? Usually, if Danny is working."

If Danny was behind the register he would let me put two beers on credit. If I needed food he was pretty lenient, I could get ten dollars' worth of groceries for a few days, but the rules for alcohol were set in stone. No booze, two beers max and paid in full next time back. It had taken me the better part of a year to earn this privilege and I didn't want to lose it.

I entered the shop to see Danny at the register, his daughter by his side.

"How was dinner?" she asked.

"Top shelf," I said.

"Dessert wasn't bad either," Tanya deadpanned for my benefit.

I got the two forties along with a reminder, "Next time, Johnny," said Danny.

"Yes sir, for sure," I answered.

We arrived at the train stop and boarded without a hitch.

"John I've got some friends up in the horseshoe Pits. They party all day, drink more in one day than most people do in a month."

"Where I was sleeping?" I asked.

"Down below. See today's the fifteenth and we're short on cash."

"So?" I asked not following.

"So, they get paid today. The booze will be flowing, it'll be insane."

"Sounds good. What do you need from me?" I asked.

"We'll show up with one of the full beers and save one for later. Give me the singles and change so we can kick in on some more."

"Here you go. Do you want the ten?"

"No you hold on to that, keep it out of sight." Tanya instructed.

Departing the train at Stanyan Street, arm in arm we descended to the front of the park.

We stopped,at a bus stop along the way, well past the main drag where maybe fifty people gathered drinking right at the front of the park, easy targets for the police sweeps possible anytime day or night.

After the beer and one last shot of brandy Tanya pulled me to my feet.

"Come on, you lush." She dragged me across the street, into the park and up the twisting trail to the pit.

The Horseshoe Pit was a large asphalt area about the size of a basketball court nestled in what was essentially a box canyon. High steep hills flanked the sides and a rock wall sealed the east end. On either side of the asphalt were horseshoe stakes in Pits of sand. The players tossed the shoes across the blacktop with the hill serving as a backstop. On the rock wall was a bas relief of a rampart stallion painted in vertical red, white and blue stripes.

The pit was a throwback to more opulent times when horseshoe-pitching tournaments were actually held on the spot. Now few people came to play and the Pits had decayed, resembling overgrown Mayan ruins more than a high society playground. Close enough to the liquor stores yet far enough off the beaten path to become the place to party.

Before we could see the revelers loud boisterous singing and shouting could be heard from the top of the hill. Rounding the corner, beer in hand, I spied a rowdy group of perhaps a half dozen guys, heads turned our way followed by a thundering, "Tanya!"

A barrage of questions quickly followed as we walked towards the pack cloistered on and around two park benches, the viewing stand of years gone by.

"Where you been?"

"Who the hell is that?"

"You got any weed?"

Tanya did the honors, introducing me as, "John from New York," which by the end of the evening earned me two new monikers, "New York John," and the one that stuck, "Johnny Jets."

We need not have worried about booze. There were bottles of every shape, brand, and size. Empties were strewn in the bushes, full bottles stacked beneath the bench -- malt liquor, wine, beer, vodka. The bounty seemed endless and it was not yet noon.

Leading the fray was Pete Cummings. He clutched a half-gallon of Jack Daniels, shouting above the ruckus in a gravelly voice. A wiry Irishman with a scruffy red beard, hair pulled back in a ponytail, a filthy blue and white bandana tied about his head. Pete appeared to be a deranged leprechaun passing out half shots from the bottle's black cap.

Tanya slipped up to me in the chaos, "So John, how do you like my friends?" she asked.

"Looks like the parties on," I answered.

"Good thing you brought some blankets, we might be here a while."

Slipping back to the festivities Tanya left me to fend for myself.

I did not realize it at the time but these guys, this place, were exactly what I had been searching for, a world where bullshitting and booze reigned supreme.

They drank without restraint, no cares in the world, living lives of drunken debauchery, a life to which I aspired.

The year before I had run out of money and luck, forced to abandon a small apartment I had near the beach, the summer weather made for a smooth transition to outdoor living. I learned quickly to adapt and survive but, except for Tanya and one or two others, I kept to myself. At the Pits I met the people who would become my surrogate family for the next few years.

I spent Thanksgiving and Christmas with these guys. I came to them when I was broke, just out the hospital or jail. They were both the reason I was able to survive and a big part of my perilous decline. When the notion of helping someone out is to buy them a bottle, the line between assisting and enabling blurs.

The cast of characters at the pit was constantly in flux. People new to town or just passing through often stayed for a few days or weeks. Others came back from months spent wandering the country or the coast, the park and specifically the pit serving as home. There were folks who lived in the neighborhood and came to let down their guard and blow off steam. There were street performers who showed up to play and sing. Men, women, a child or two, two dogs, and though I've forgotten the names of most of the people, I can still remember theirs, Lizard and Roscoe. It was glimpse of what the Haight and the Summer of Love must have been like thirty-five years before.

The core group during my days in the Pits consisted of Pete Cummings, Kenny Nelson, Bob Pardini, Jim Sweney, Steve the Cab Driver, Purnell "Slim" Potter, and two who became like brothers to me, Pat Hosteter and Samuel Perry Clarke.

A big man in khaki shorts tied with a scrap of rope, and a bold print Hawaiian shirt stepped in front of me and stuck out a meaty paw. "Name's Pat," he boomed. "Call me Hoss."

At six foot three and two hundred forty pounds, Hoss was solid, dense like a defensive tackle. Everything about him was large, my hand disappeared in his catcher's mitt sized paw. We talked as the sun bore down intermittently between the swaying branches and pine boughs. He told me he had worked for years as a hod carrier, a mason tender responsible for keeping five bricklayers stocked with mortar and brick or block. The mortar came from a small gas powered mixer he filled with cement, sand and water. An iced down six pack never far from his side, amid the roar of the eight horse power Briggs and Stratton the concrete congealing in the spinning mixer he would lug the block to where it was needed, and then return to haul the mortar in wheel barrows and buckets back to the masons.

Bricklayers were often paid by the piece for their efforts so they worked at a blistering pace. Pat's job was to keep up, keep them moving. To say it was hard work was far more than an understatement, it was blood money, the results of his labors apparent in his physique and demeanor.

We took swigs on the forty I had brought when Tanya reappeared grabbing the bottle, "Having fun, Johnny Boy?" she asked, clearly enjoying the party herself.

"It's great, how 'bout you?" I responded.

"Just go easy on the liquor. These guys are pros," she whispered in my ear and pecked my cheek.

"I'll stick with the beer," I reassured her.

"Did Tanya just kiss you?" Hoss asked.

"Yeah, something wrong?"

"Nothing, just never saw her act, you know, lovey-dovey."

"That wasn't lovey-dovey," I responded.

"For her it was," said Big Pat.

"Come on!" someone shouted so loud beside me that I jumped.

Pete stood with a capful of JD extended to me. I downed the shot, quickly dismissing my promise to Tanya as Hoss snatched the bottle by the neck from Pete's hand. He downed a huge gulp and wiped his face with the back of his hand.

"WHOOOOO!!" he shouted loud and long, a war whoop I would hear many times.

"Hey that's my bottle!" Pete yelled.

"I've got the next one!" Hoss hollered unzipping the pack at his feet to reveal not one but two more half gallons.

"Holy Shit," was all I could muster.

The party continued for two more days. Tanya and I slept, warm and dry, in my spot on top of the hill. I ran empty cans and bottles from around the park and nearby streets to the recycling center on the opposite side of Sharon Meadow for a little money. Tanya asked for the ten and gave it to Pat who took ours along with five or six others to get more booze. He always came back with twice what the money would buy so no one asked any questions.

Somewhere around the end of Day Three Tanya and I took a break from the raucous celebration.

I dug through my pockets and came up with a buck and a half. "Hey T, you have any money?

Tanya dug in her purse hoping to find some treasure she had missed.

"Ah ha!, Look what I found, Johnny Boy," she blurted holding a small bag of what looked like coins.

"Quarters?" I asked.

"Better," she said. "Bus tokens, a dollar twenty-five a piece and there's ten."

"Jackpot! Where do we turn them into cash, Franks?"

"Yep, I'm tired of all the noise. Want to head back to the beach?" she asked.

"You read my mind."

45

We returned to the Pits, enjoying a few pops as we said our goodbyes. I climbed the hill to pack up camp and head home. Tanya joined me at the top. We stood at the precipice to wave a dramatic goodbye but no one looked up, the party, in its third day, still in high gear.

Frank's was along the way to the N-Judah, our chariot home. Tanya burst through the door like she owned the place, heading straight to Frank standing in his hollow.

Frank took one look, raised his eyes and hands to the sky, shouting, "What? What have I done?"

"I missed you too. How much for these?" she asked, dangling the bag of tokens.

"Five dollars," Frank answered.

"Five dollars, are you kidding? This is America, buddy, there's twelve fifty here," she negotiated.

"What do you want?"

"Four beers," she stated decisively.

"Three," Frank countered.

"Deal," Tanya agreed.

"Go get them," he relented.

As we left the store Frank called me back, "You with her now?"

"Sure looks that way," I answered proudly.

Frank just looked to the floor shaking his head.

*   *   *

Thus began the best summer I spent in Golden Gate Park. Tanya and I returned to the thorn fortress, slipping into a routine best described as comfortable. Increasingly aware of Tanya's reluctance to wake early, I dressed and booted up in silence, leaving at daybreak to scour the beach and surrounding neighborhoods for recycling, the cans and bottles I collected our main revenue stream.

I made it my business to know where the large blue recycling pails would be each day. Mondays, they were close to the beach and on the hills by Sutro Heights, Tuesdays a little farther east, 35th to 45th Avenue along Fulton, Wednesdays on the park's south side. Raiding the bins was illegal but the three times the cops pinched me I explained it was the least illegal thing I could think of to survive. My earnestness, coupled with the undeniable work ethic demonstrated by my cartful of recycling, had kept me out of trouble so far.

I began most days with a run around the golf course before the first duffers rose. The course sold beer in cans and plastic bottles and if I was the first one there the pails at each tee were normally full. I started at the clubhouse, covering each hole of the nine-hole par three. This morning the yield was plentiful, lots of cans, currently worth one dollar a pound. At the seventh hole I spied a Heineken by the leg of a bench, unopened on top of two folded dollar bills. This was already looking like a great day. I snatched a rake from the sand trap to use at our camp and doubled back for a quick check on Tanya. She lay cuddling some brandy from the night before. I grabbed our

47

last forty, put the Heineken by the bed, and dropped the rake at the base of a pine. Hitting the road, bags in hand to see what else the day might bring.

At the Safeway supermarket I found a roller -- a shopping cart not equipped with an electronic brake to prevent theft -- and tied the bags to its chrome basket. I timed my arrival at the beach with the first rays of daylight needed to scan the sand.

I loved to recycle the beach. Like so many treasure hunters I never knew what I might find. Every day was good but weekends, like today, were especially bountiful. Weekends brought parties, bonfires and and happy, inebriated revelers likely to leave anything in the sand. I had found money, jewelry, wallets, cell phones, and cameras -- all easily sold or, if possible, returned minus the cash for a well-deserved reward. The key, as always, was to get there first; in this case, the early bird really did get the worm -- hopefully floating in the bottom of an unopened bottle of tequila.

I worked north to south along the concrete boardwalk checking the trash cans perched at each stairway opening. The procedure was to descend to the beach, search the sand around the smoldering ashes then move to the next opening. Practice enabled me to tell from a long distance what would likely be profitable. People are creatures of habit and intoxicated people are creatures of bad habits. If I saw a cardboard beer carton but not enough empties to go with it I would dig where the sand appeared to be disturbed, and, more often than not, I would find the balance of the bottles and cans buried full in the sand.

This morning I was in my glory. The recycling was excellent and I was ground scoring left and right. I worked quickly to beat my competitors to the punch keeping a watchful eye for anyone else picking the beach. A dozen assorted beers, a half pint of vodka -- Royal Gate, the cheap stuff -- open as if someone choked down a swig then decided the rot gut was not worth the effort, three bottles of chardonnay, two with the corks and seals intact, the third barely touched.

Few can fully appreciate the unbridled joy of an alcoholic finding free booze, *lots* of free booze. The scene in *Leaving Las Vegas* where Nicholas Cage gleefully fills his shopping cart with bottles bought with his severance pay is as close as I can come. Only someone who has endured the morning shakes and countless hours in AA meetings can understand the wondrous abandon in this moment.

I was on the beach, plenty of beer, getting some money together, joggers and surfers just beginning to appear, thanking me for cleaning the sand. This was what Jimmy Buffett sang about. This was paradise.

As I passed the Beach Chalet, an upscale bar restaurant opposite Ocean Beach, I spied a familiar silhouette poking around near the dumpster.

"Sammy!" I shouted.

Sam spun sharply, suspiciously eyeing those passing by to see who had the nerve to call his name. Across the divided thoroughfare I was unmistakable at the helm of my shopping cart, bags bulging on either side.

"Johnny Boy!" he hollered, sprinting through traffic, oblivious to the screeching tires and blaring horns.

"You got a drink, man?" was his first question. "I'm shakin' like a snitch at a gangsta party."

"Here you go," I said handing him the open wine, which disappeared in two monstrous swigs.

"Anything stronger?" he asked hopefully. "I am not a well man."

"Hold on, I'm loaded," I told him, digging through the empties for the Royal Gate and a Bud to chase it.

"Oh yeah, brother! That's what I'm talking about." He cracked the beer and took a pull of vodka followed by a gulp of Bud. Sam coughed, swallowed hard, then gagged a little but he held everything down. "Mother's milk," he sputtered between gasps.

Like the Horseshoe Pit to the east, the beach along the park's west end had its own cast of characters, among them Samuel Perry Clarke or Sammy C., a displaced New Yorker, like myself, now a fixture in Golden Gate Park.

Depending on who was doing the counting there were anywhere from a few hundred to a few thousand homeless wandering the streets of San Francisco, and a good percentage called the park home. We all kind of knew each other, if not directly then through the homeless grapevine. We knew who the drunks and dope fiends were, who was a snitch, who to trust and who to avoid. The bond between Sam and I formed quickly thanks to uncanny similarities in our past and current circumstances.

We were both from New York, Sam from Staten Island, I from Long Island. We'd both been carpenters, union carpenters in fact, losing good paying jobs to our insatiable thirst. We'd both wound up here, neighbors in the woods, three thousand miles from home. We had met several years before attempting to get sober in one of many programs and detox centers around San Francisco, only to end up again and again right where we started. Prior to November 2, 2005, he was one of only a handful people who had seen me sober west of the Mississippi.

Sam was only about five foot eight but tipped the scales at 180 pounds of muscle. He had a sharp wit and killer sense of humor. He was tough, good in a fight, loyal to the core, the kind of guy you wanted by your side walking down a dark alley. Living on the streets alliances were key and Sam and I had saved each other's asses more than once.

Sam surveyed the loaded buggy, lifting each bag to gauge the weight.

"Good start, huh, Johnny," Sammy said.

"Yeah, been lucky no one else was out today." I picked up an empty bag and hit the beach.

Sam stood guard over my cart during my forays to the sand, allowing me to move quicker, work faster. I finished my run in under an hour, capping the cart with four full Coronas and a lime stuffed in a cardboard six-pack holder at the Lincoln Street end where the Mexicans usually partied.

I reversed course and headed back to Safeway's parking lot, where the recycling center opened at ten. Sam tagged along to help me. The total haul was close to forty bucks and I gave Sam a ten, more for keeping me company than anything else.

"Where you headed?" Sam asked.

"I have to meet Tanya up by the golf course," I said, not wanting to share our relationship status or the location of the camp.

51

"I heard about that. You serious with her?"

"I guess," I replied. "We live in a tree. How serious can it be?"

"Huh," he grunted, thinking it over. "Just remember two broken wheels can't fix each other."

We headed to Blockhead Joe's. Sammy picked up a beer and a paper, I grabbed Tanya's coffee and an ice cold forty before heading up the hill to 43rd Avenue, the park entrance closest to the camp.

Sam and I walked to edge of North Lake where I stashed the buggy in a little hollow behind the hedges I had begun to refer to as my garage. Rollers were good to have and I wanted to hang on to this one.

I found myself at a crossroads. Sam clearly had no place to go, Tanya was waiting a quarter mile away in what was easily the best camp I had ever found. A thousand questions flew through my head.

Should I share the spot's location out of friendship? Although she knew Sammy, how would Tanya react to unsolicited company? Would this throw a monkey wrench in the relatively quiet few weeks I had enjoyed?

I decided to go with the flow and head back to camp. If Tanya threw a fit Sam would have to find another spot, but for today, at least, I hoped we could all be friends.

Sam helped me carry the newly found booty along the trails back to the camp. We paused alongside the thorn bushes.

"Shhhh," I hissed, holding a finger across my lips.

The sound of the radio wafted through the prickly underbrush.

"In there?" Sam asked as if I had suggested walking through fire.

"Just follow me and be careful."

"Incoming," I warned. Adding, "And I've got company."

Tanya had the camp shipshape as we popped free of the thorns.

"Hello boys," she said timidly at first, and then recognizing Sammy burst into, "Sammy C! You old pirate! Where you been hiding?"

"Hey Tanya," said Sam. "Heard you were shackin' up with this bum. How's he treatin' ya?"

"Just wonderfully, thank you," Tanya replied in her best British accent.

"Yeah, he's good people," Sam replied.

"You know it," I added.

"What's in the bag?" Tanya queried.

"Presents, my dear."

"You leave me this one?" she asked, raising the Heineken.

"Of course. I found it on the golf course along with the day's first two bucks."

"That's mine," bemoaned Sam. "I musta left it there last night."

I laughed out loud. "Sammy, in the three years I've known you, you've,

A) never played golf

B) never spent three bucks on a twelve ounce beer, and

C) never put your money anywhere but in your pocket or the liquor store register."

Sam shrugged. "Can't kill a guy for tryin'. Oh, my fuckin' head!"

Looking more than a little dizzy, he plopped in a pile of pine needles, leaned up against one of the biggest pines, spun off the top of his forty, and unfolded his paper.

"What about meee!" groaned Tanya, doing her best to imitate Sammy.

I handed her the coffee, adding, "It might be cold, it took us a while to get here."

"I'll warm it up," she said, pulling the remains of last night's E&J from beneath the pile of blankets.

"Holding out on me, eh?" I kidded.

She spiked the coffee, stirring in some cream and sugar, "Irish coffee."

I began digging in the bag, standing each bottle and can one at a time in a row for Tanya to admire.

"You found all this just this morning?" Tanya asked.

"Yep," I answered proudly.

"Why on Earth would you buy more?" she asked.

"The beers are all warm and I can't take wine in the morning."

"Unless that's all there is," Sammy chimed in without taking his eyes off his paper.

"He knows you like a book, Johnny boy," commented Tanya. "Did you cash in already too?"

"Yeah we have almost thirty left, gave Sam a ten too."

"You didn't give me anything, I earned it," squawked Sammy.

"He stands in a different spot and it costs me twenty five an hour," I groused.

"Thirty bucks plus all this loot, I'd say we did OK," Tanya interjected.

"What's this 'we' stuff? You got a mouse in your pocket?" Sam chided.

"Fine, I'll do the cooking. How does that sound?" Tanya asked.

"Sounds great, I'm starved," I replied. "You coming Sam?"

"Nah, you guys mind if I take a booze snooze?"

I looked to Tanya who tossed Sam a blanket. "Make sure you hide the blankets if you leave."

"Stealth, Sammy. Clandestine. Unseen," I reiterated to protect the spot.

"Yeah, yeah I heard you, now let me get some shuteye."

"Don't snore too loud," Tanya added.

"How the hell will I know how loud I'm snoring?" Sam muttered, his snores filling the air before we cleared the brush.

We headed for Safeway to shop for the day's main meal. Slipping between two registers Tanya mused for a moment tapping her chin with her right index finger, her left hand theatrically mounted to her hip.

"How about burgers?" she asked. "Big juicy ones, with fries?"

"Let's go with chips? Fries are too hard to cook in the woods."

"Chips it is," Tanya decided. "I'll get the meat and buns."

I headed to the deli counter, adding a Caesar salad to the budding feast. "Could I get some dressing?" I asked sheepishly.

With a smile, the Asian woman behind the glass counter filled a small bag with packets of all kinds of different condiments. We returned to camp with a bag of ice for the beers and headed off leaving a still snoring Sammy C. Skirting the golf course we arrived again at the duck pond. I lit the fire and Tanya set to cooking. I opened a beer and began whipping up a sauce from the packets of ketchup, mayo and mustard; now was as good a time as any to broach the subject of Sammy.

I started slowly, cautiously wading into these uncharted waters. "I think Sam might want to stick around our spot, the cops ran everyone out from behind the Chalet last night."

"Well those people are morons anyway, screaming, yelling, fighting, making a huge mess of the park. The only reason they're not waste deep in trash is you pick up the recycling every day."

"Still, he has no place to go. What would you think of letting him stay by us?" I asked, still not sure if I even wanted this.

"I'm okay with it as long as he stays down front, we can move up the hill away from the trail and set up the tent," said Tanya sorting things out in her head as she spoke. I was amazed at her acceptance and ingenuity, she had chosen to make the best of this ambiguous situation.

"Never hurts to help somebody out," she added.

"What about 'No good deed ever goes unpunished?'" I asked in response.

"That too," said Tanya.

"Karma?" I offered.

"Sort of. I believe what goes round comes round but I don't think good people always get what they deserve or that bad ones always get screwed in the end. Sometimes nice guys really do finish last."

"I guess, but I think there is a purpose, a reason everything happens. We're just too wrapped up in all our drama to see the big picture."

"Well, right now, my picture is filled with hungry ducks." She swiped a bun from the top of the pile and walked off to feed her feathered friends.

We ate lunch along the shore, packed the leftovers, then made our way back to camp. Arriving at the twisting trail through the thorns, we snuck into the den.

Sam was still sound asleep prompting Tanya to yell, "See, I told you he would be fine without a sitter," loud enough to wake the dead and Sammy as well.

The mound of blankets half covered in leaves moved a little from side to side. I began to smile.

"What do you call a man with no arms and no legs hiding beneath a pile of leaves?" I asked Tanya.

She looked at me quizzically, "What?"

"What do you call a man with no arms and no legs hiding beneath a pile of leaves?"

"I get that -- what do you call him?"

"Russell."

"Idiot," she said with a smirk, as if my half-assed comments had amused perhaps half her brain.

"What fuckin' time is it?" asked the leaf covered pile of blankets.

"Six thirty, time to make the donuts," I replied.

The blanket flew across the ground as Sam leaped into the world of the living. "No shit, it's morning."

"No Sam, six thirty Saturday evening, you've been sleeping seven hours," I said. I handed him the bag of food and began fishing through the ice for the Coronas. I dug out three and dropped the lime on the stump to slice it.

"Great I'm starvin'," he rumbled as he tore into the chow.

"Damage control," Sammy announced between gargantuan bites, crumbs of meat and bread falling from his mouth as spoke. He pulled a small woman's compact from the pocket of his jacket, stared into the mirror pushing his hair back and forth with his fingers.

"Christ, looks like I've been combing my hair with fire crackers," he noted. "Tanya, you got a brush?"

"You got bugs?" she asked.

"No," Sam roared indignantly.

"Then I have a comb, no brush." She handed him her comb.

Sam struggled to comb his hair with his left hand while holding the mirror in his right. Giving up he returned the comb and pulled the Royal Gate from his jacket. He took a short pull gagging and coughing but getting it down.

"Damn, I need a shower," Sam added.

"Wouldn't hurt, you smell like a rabbit hutch," replied Tanya sniffing Sam.

"Put this in the ice," he said passing the bottle. "These too," he added, a beer magically appearing from each of his jacket's front pockets. The folded ten-dollar bill fell to the ground.

"Where did this come from?" Sam asked.

"You earned it, remember?"

"I must have been really fucked up."

"Ya think?" Tanya asked.

I plugged the Corona's long necks with a chunk of lime, covered the end with my thumb and flipped each one over and back. I handed Tanya a beer.

"Gimme one, Johnny," said Sam.

"On the way," I replied.

"Patience is a virtue," added Tanya.

"Sure, you already got one."

"Ladies first," said Tanya getting in the last jab.

I repeated the process twice, handed Sammy a beer, and took a swig on mine.

"Johnny, I gotta pee," Tanya announced after one particularly big chug.

I started to stand. "Come on, I'm a big girl just give me the key."

She walked over and kissed me. I handed over the precious key.

"Be back in ten," she said, disappearing into the thorns, radio in one hand, Corona swaying beneath the other.

"Hey, Johnny," Sam asked as soon as she was out of earshot. "You got room here for one more?"

"Yeah Sam, you can stay."

"Tanya's cool with that too?"

"Yes, we talked about it this afternoon."

"Saw it coming huh?"

"Well I been there too, so just stay down front here and we'll move back up the hill."

"I got some blankets and shit over by Black Joe's log. I'll go get cleaned up and bring them back in a couple hours," Sam said.

"Bring some more beer," I adjured.

"Least I can do," Sam replied and disappeared into the thorns.

Now alone I lifted the boulder camouflage tarp and dug the tent from the pile of supplies. Heading to the rear of the campsite I picked a level spot to set up, using the rake procured from the golf course to clear the ground and dig free a few stones. The next step was bedding, I piled pine needles high and staked the tent on top. I tried unsuccessfully to raise the top of the dome myself. In the distance I could hear the radio playing and knew Tanya was not far off.

"I'm home, Johnny boy," she announced just before coming into view.

"Hello dear. Everything come out all right?" I asked.

"Very funny. What are you up to now?"

"Trying to set up camp for real. Want to give me a hand?" I asked, trying to appeal to her sense of teamwork.

"Can't you ever be still?"

"When they close the lid on me. Plenty of time to catch up then," I added.

Tanya shuffled to the corner opposite me. We wrestled with the fiberglass poles for a few minutes, and suddenly the tent popped into shape, standing in all its glory at the back of our site.

"Wow, this is big," commented Tanya, slipping inside.

I grabbed another beer and made my way around the base of the tent, pounding in stakes with a rock.

"Eight by eight," I answered, standing to catch a breath and slug down some brew.

Tanya poked around inside. "I can stand up in here," she announced. "Well in the middle at least."

The tent had indeed been a bargain, all the parts accounted for, no rips or tears, missing the rain fly but that was to be expected.

Tanya swept the floor inside with an old towel.

"Smells a little," she noted, sniffing like a rabbit.

"It'll air out in a day or two," I replied.

"What about the tarp?" Tanya asked, pointing to the crumpled brown tarp on the ground.

"That's step two, but I'll need some rope," I answered.

"Would Safeway have it?"

"They probably have clothesline; that would do. Wanna take a walk?"

"Lead the way," she said.

We tidied up the camp, grabbed four beers for the trip and headed to the store. Before making our way down the hill, I circled the camp, checking the perimeter from the surrounding trails. The tent was visible at only one small spot. Fashioning a blind by weaving some dead branches into the live ones solved that problem, rendering the tent nearly invisible.

Tanya admired my work. "Nicely done."

"That's the idea dear, you can't see a thing," I added, adjusting the coverage a little more. "Off we go."

The lights of the Safeway parking lot were just buzzing to life as we reached the door. In the hardware section I found a fifty-foot roll of black nylon cord. Tanya bumped my elbow with a small whisk-broom that clipped strategically into its dustpan.

"Its seven bucks, but we need it, and it's so cute," she commented.

We exited the store ten dollars lighter but pleased at outfitting our new camp properly.

"Know what?" Tanya asked. "We just spent ten bucks on something other than beer."

"Will wonders never cease? Now give me a beer," I said.

"It's always beer with you -- beer, beer, beer, beer, beer," she sang in a polka rhythm.

"That's right, 'Have Beer, Am Happy.' Chisel it on my tombstone."

We moved down the trail behind the Beach Chalet, the gleam of the flashlight leading the way.

"Where'd Sammy go?" asked Tanya.

"To get his stuff by Black Joe's log. Think we should check it out?

"Sure," said Tanya.

Situated between the soccer fields and the Great Highway sat Black Joe's Log. Joe had manned it for years. Over time it had become to the stragglers of the park's west end what "Cheers" was to Boston. Joe himself could best be described as a Renaissance bum, spending most of his days reading atop the log and all of his nights partying beside it. Joe's wrists and fingers were adorned with ornate silver bracelets and rings. He wore a black leather baseball cap and Blues Brothers glasses at all times, exuding a Miles Davis vibe with his slight build, and a raspy, smoky voice that grew less coherent with each drink..

"Who's that comin' in," he shouted, spying the light inching towards the log.

"Johnny Joe," I shouted back.

"And Tanya," the voice behind me chimed in.

"Well come on in, just lose the light."

I killed the light; in seconds our eyes adjusted to the darkness. Joe stuck out a hand and wrapped an arm around my shoulder. He spun me aside and gave Tanya a big hug.

"You two know each other?" I asked dumbfounded.

"How long we know each other now, Tanya? Ten? Fifteen years?"

"At least. Been a while though, Joe, probably a year," she answered, slipping from his grasp.

"What the fuck, you two a couple now?" Joe asked earnestly.

"Couple of what?" I puzzled in return.

"Where's your light?" Joe barked with a grin.

I passed the flashlight to him. He dug in the tall beach grass growing behind the log.

"Ah ha!" he shouted. "The bar is open!" A half-gallon of Absolut hung from his hand.

"We can build the chaser right in." Joe poured out about a third of a two-liter Seven-Up and filled it back up with the vodka. He took a huge pull and roared again, "Oh yes, the bar is open!"

We sat with Joe laughing, singing and drinking his vodka.

"You see Sammy at all, Joe?" I asked.

"Came by a while back. Went over to Mark's to take a shower."

"Black Mark's?" I asked. We called him Black Mark because, like Joe, he was black and, also like Joe, more than one of the gang had the same name.

"That's the one," he replied. "Said he was staying up by you."

"Yeah, one more ain't gonna hurt too much."

"You got room?" Joe asked with a nod towards Tanya.

"Sure, it's a big enough park."

"That it is, Johnny. Just don't let nobody cramp your style."

Tanya was fiddling with the radio and soon Sam Cooke was crooning "Another Saturday Night." I sat beside Tanya and gave her a kiss on the cheek.

"What was that for?" she asked.

"I got somebody...," I replied.

"You're weird," she declared.

We stayed at the log for another hour or so, Joe out drinking us by a good clip, getting louder by the swig. A half dozen new hobos had joined the festivities when a look from Tanya told me it was time to go. I slipped on the backpack, we said a hasty goodnight then wove our way through the desolate paths to the golf course -- a straight shot maybe half a mile across would bring us right to our camp.

"Hold up, John," Tanya said, sitting to rest on the yellow bench a top the ninth hole. As I sat down beside her, she pulled a twenty-ounce bottle from her bag. "A nightcap from Joe."

"What a surprise, more booze."

She took a short sip. "Oh my God is this strong!"

I took a taste myself, even after a few hours drinking it tasted like pure vodka. "Let's put a cork in that 'til we get home."

"Or we might not make it home," giggled Tanya.

Crossing the manicured course was easy; literally a walk in the park, but the last two hundred yards was a different story. We used the light intermittently, turning it on to find a clear path then dousing it so no one could see our route. Soon we stood before the tent. I stacked the blankets while Tanya combed out her hair. A few minutes later the bed was finished and we scampered inside.

"Want some?" she offered, holding the nightcap.

"Too strong. I'll get some more soda tomorrow. How about some wine?" I asked pulling a full bottle from the stash bag.

"Lovely," she replied. I pulled the cork and handed her the bottle. "A toast then, to living indoors."

"In flaps," I corrected.

"What are you talking about now?" she asked.

"Houses have doors, tents have flaps," I stated a bit smugly.

"Ah yes!" she cheered. "To living in flaps."

"To flaps with screens!" I bellowed, raising the bottle high until I caught a whiff of my armpit. "God, do I need a shower."

Tanya sniffed at my chest. "Lord yes, you too smell like a rabbit hutch."

"Where is the water?"

"Don't use it all," instructed Tanya. "I need some left to drink."

I left the tent and hurried through a birdbath with the water from our jug. It wasn't freezing, but cold enough to make me rush through the process. Drying quickly with my t-shirt, I dove back into the tent.

"Better?" I asked now zipping the tent flaps tight.

"Much better. Cover your eyes."

I did and Tanya sprayed a blast of perfume over me.

"Tanya, what the hell? Now I smell like a two dollar whore!"

"Hey, this stuff's expensive." She sprayed a dab on each wrist and sniffed. "Smells great too."

"Not on me!" I countered.

"Better than a rabbit hutch."

"True, true," I acquiesced.

I slid into bed beside her. She snuggled up tight to me, the glow between us warming the tent.

"You getting up early tomorrow?" she asked, hoping the answer would be no.

"Yeah, it's Sunday, but I can still make some money and get a head start on Monday."

"You work too hard."

"I don't mind recycling, it's kind of like Forrest Gump's chocolates -- you never know what you're gonna get."

"Johnny, you could hit the lottery and you would still be pushing that stupid cart."

"That's right and I would have a big house with a three car garage, two for the cars and one for the buggy. I would get up every day and push my buggy down our enormous circular driveway then head straight for our neighbors' cans."

"I would like that," she said quietly.

"You wouldn't be embarrassed?" I asked.

"Hell yes, but for a car and a house with a circular driveway, I'd let you push your happy ass to L.A. Hell, I'd pack you lunch."

"Could I get a lunch pail? A big Ralph Cramden one that looks like a mailbox and opens down the middle?" I said in a mock pleading tone.

"You would be a sight," said Tanya, imagining the scene, "Leaving a million dollar home at the crack of dawn, lunch pail in the kiddies' seat of the buggy, shorts, sunglasses and Timberland boots, off to raid the neighbors' blue bins."

"I would like it," I replied somewhat defensively.

"I know, that's what scares me."

We leaned back quietly sipping the wine, until the distinctive sound of a branch snapping brought me quickly to my feet. It was faint but someone was definitely outside, a second crack told me they were getting closer.

I crossed my index finger over my lips, the universal sign for "dummy up now." Tanya responded by silently passing me my knife. I took it slowly, twisting the wine cork off its pointy chrome pigtail. Slipping stealthily out of the tent I listened intently, scanning the perimeter for movement.

When you live outside you grow acutely aware of any inappropriate, unusual sound. A squirrel foraging in a tree sounds like a rhino crashing through the thickets of Africa. Even while sound asleep a snap no louder than the click of a pen would send me scrambling for weapons left at the ready, a knife buried to its hilt in the dirt, or a bat tucked invisibly beneath the edge of a bedroll. My personal favorite was a golf club, its weighted head provided the concentrated force of a death blow hammer. Knives were mainly for threatening, to actually use one you needed to get in close, too close, the result often fatal. A swift swing to the kneecaps with a Mashie produced a silent, crippling blow, a busted kneecap or shin the extent of the damage. The 5-iron had the added advantage of not being classified as a deadly weapon. If the source of the noise turned out to be wearing a blue uniform the sight of a blade would immediately cause him to point his gun at me. A vagrant with a golf club could pass for a confused Jack Nicklaus or Tiger Woods depending on how many strange women he had slept with.

The rake leaning against the pine would work tonight. I dropped to a crouch, digging the knife into the soft soil. The sound came again, this time from the opposite direction. Someone was circling the camp. No light meant it wasn't the cops or rangers, they weren't dumb enough to wander the woods at night without one. I turned to Tanya now kneeling in the front of the tent. My warrior princess had finished the wine, the bottle now a bludgeon gripped tightly by the neck in her clenched fist. The sound came again followed by a desperate drunken cry.

"McHugh, I know you're in there! I can't get into this fuckin' place!"

"Sammy?" asked Tanya, a smile beginning to creep across her face.

"Who else?" I responded, then yelling to Sam, "Quiet down, I'll get a light."

I shined the flashlight on the path that split the thorns. "That's the entrance."

I heard Sam move to the light, slashing briefly across its beam as he wove his way into our den. Shaved and showered, hair tousled but washed, he staggered to my side to drop his bundles at my feet.

"Young man, I told you to be in by midnight. That's it, you're grounded!" Tanya scolded.

"Hi Tanya," Sam said with a shy, dopey grin, eyes glassy like some precocious leprechaun. "I brought beer, guys!" He held a bag aloft, staggering a little to the right like the weight of the bag was pulling him down.

"Good man, open one up," I ordered.

We passed the bottle. The beer was bitter and cold in biting contrast to the wine. Sammy squatted down, tottering a little before falling flat on his back.

"Put that boy to bed, Johnny boy," declared Tanya, crouching to crawl back into the tent.

I gathered Sammy's things as he struggled mightily to return to his feet. I barely got the first quilt down when he staggered forward and fell hard across its center, a loud thump like a bass drum emanating from his chest as the air rushed from his lungs. It had to hurt, but he was far too drunk to care.

"'Night, Sam," I half whispered, covering him with the remaining blankets as he grabbed the beer in the bag tight to his chest.

Tanya waited in the tent. I parted the flaps with the open beer and motioned it to her.

"No thanks, I'll just have to pee again."

"You do that quite nicely, really," I complimented.

"What? Pee? Well, it's not my first night in the woods, you know."

I took one last pull and capped the bottle. We lay quietly in each other's arms staring at the nylon ceiling.

"Wanna hear something funny?" Tanya asked hesitantly.

"Sure, tell me," I prodded.

"You can't go blabbing this around," she added. "One night, about a year ago, I was down in North Beach and I really had to pee, I mean my eyeballs were floating. I tried the bars and restaurants but they were all full so I couldn't get in. So I snuck off to the back corner of this parking lot -- I had on a long coat so I could just squat down and no one could tell."

"That's why you always wear long coats? Even in June?"

"Can I finish please? You're always interrupting me. Anyway, I look around, the coast is clear so I squat down, all of a sudden the car directly across from me turns the headlights on."

"No," I whisper.

"Uh huh, so I lift my hand and flip him the bird, then a red light on the dash starts spinning around, bouncing off all the cars and the wall behind me, like a damn laser light show. Since I don't stand up right away he hits the siren!"

"No shit, what did you do?" I asked transfixed.

"What could I do? You can't stop in midstream, so I finished up, fixed my clothes, turned and gave him a curtsey. You know a big sweeping one, like they do on Broadway."

"Did he ticket you?" I asked.

"That bastard was laughing so hard he probably peed his own pants!" she blurted out between giggles.

"Let me up before I pee mine." Now we were the ones laughing.

I returned to the tent, zipping the screen tight. "We need a coffee can or something. It's gonna stink if we just keep going in one spot."

"Just dig a hole, Daniel Boone," she chastised. "Now get to sleep, no more potty talk."

"Night T."

"Night John, love you."

"Love you too." And more and more I really did.

The night ended too quickly; soon the ravens were cawing loudly in the tops of the trees. A can of Chef Boyardee beef ravioli hacked open with my knife served as breakfast, hardly proper fare for a Sunday morning but essential nonetheless.

A big problem with an alcohol-fueled, nomadic existence was you quickly lost the will to eat. At first hunger was a constant companion, but by day two or three, the booze's empty calories replaced real food. By the end of a month, if you weren't careful, eating became a nuisance, getting in the way of what you really wanted to do. The result was weight loss, fatigue, wicked hangovers, finally the dreaded DT's as the body quickly faltered, deteriorated, disintegrated. Anyone who survived for more than a few weeks outdoors realized the need to eat at least one full meal each day, wherever the food came from -- stamps, soup kitchens, church basement handouts. It didn't matter, you had to eat.

Again I hit the golf course, followed by the beach. The pickings weren't as good as Saturday but I had a full load, another five beers, and a Styrofoam cooler packed with ice and two packs of hot links. I stashed the cartful of glass containers in my "garage" and carried the cans and plastics in two bags knotted together over my left shoulder, the cooler balanced high atop my right.

"A cooler, huh? Good score, Johnny boy," said Sammy, sipping his wake-up as I entered the camp.

"Yeah, still got some ice and these." I held up a package of links for Sam's approval.

"Nice. Didn't happen to get a paper, did ya?"

"No, Tanya's got the bank. Is she up yet?"

"Haven't seen her. I stopped at Joe's log on the way back last night. Man, it was on."

"Yeah, we were there too, took off when things started to get rough."

A puffy, sleepy face surrounded by a mop of black hair poked through the tent flaps.

"Good Morning, dear," I crowed.

"What's so good about it? Did you get the coffee?" replied Tanya.

"No, you have all the cash."

"Oh hell, why didn't you wake me?"

I shot Sammy a bewildered glance. "Mizz Rains, you surely must be kidding."

She raised an eyebrow, considering my predicament, "I guess you're right."

"We'll go right now. I want a paper," Sam chimed in. "I'll even buy. Just take it off the rent."

"Give me a second," I said, packing the cooler with all the leftover beer and wine along with the potent nightcap.

"Where's the brandy, T?"

"You stay away from that -- it's for my coffee!"

"Do you want it in the ice?"

She stuck her head out again, hair combed, face still puffy, "What ice? Isn't it melted? Oh, a cooler! Now we're really living."

"Stick with me, kid," I told her. "I'm going places."

"Yeah, to Joe's and hurry back," was her terse reply.

"Want a beer, Sam?"

"No, I'm good," he replied.

"COFFEE!!" came the roar from the tent, sending Sam and I scurrying for the safety of the woods.

Exiting the park at 43rd we completed the familiar walk -- one block down, one block over, returning home with the paper, two forties and Tanya's coffee all courtesy of Sammy C.

"Should we throw the coffee in first like a piece of raw meat?" Sam asked as we neared the camp.

"Probably, we don't have a whip or chair."

Tanya however had other ideas. Now perfectly composed, she moved about the campsite tidying up, a task she repeated nearly every day and actually seemed to enjoy.

"Neat as a pin," she commented with a clap of her hands.

Sam handed Tanya the java and in return received a kiss on the cheek.

"Tanya," he said sheepishly, turning his head to hide his blushing face.

"Big, tough ex-con from New York, my ass," I teased.

Tanya set to work fixing her coffee, Sam watching the process intently.

"Brandy in there too?" he asked, opening the first forty.

"Irish Coffee," she replied, followed by the first lip smacking sip. "Give me all that stuff."

Taking the garbage from Sam she stuffed it into one of my large plastic recycling bags. "This is for trash!" she commanded loudly.

Sam sat back to read his paper. In between slugs of beer I packed the backpack. "Should we bring a few beers?"

"How many have we got?" Tanya asked.

"Maybe a dozen," I answered.

"Take four, leave the rest."

"Hot Links?" I asked.

"Where did you get those?" she asked.

"Found them this morning with the cooler. Two packs. Take one, leave one?"

"Sounds good."

"Blankets?"

"Sure, take a few, just in case."

Sam paused from his reading, "Where you guys goin?"

"I've got to go to Kezar to cash in, then probably to the Pits," I answered.

"Mind if I tag along?" Sam asked.

"Not at all, we wouldn't think about leaving without you," replied Tanya.

The packing continued.

"Radio?" Tanya asked.

"Check." I replied.

"Flashlight?"

"Check."

"This is too funny," laughed Tanya.

"What?" I asked.

"We're packing like it's a moon shot!"

"Yeah, I guess. Wine?"

"Check," she snickered again.

I spun the pack onto my shoulders. Sam killed the first forty and slipped the second inside his Carhart jacket.

"And, away we go!" he shouted, accompanied by his best Jackie Gleason shuffle.

The N Judah pulled to our stop and we snuck aboard. No inspectors worked Sundays so we each opened a short beer, enjoying the climb from the ocean to the Haight. Tanya and I left the train first, exiting at UCSF to head down the hill to the recycling center, one of the few in San Francisco open on Sunday. Sam stayed on one more stop, getting off at Stanyan Street to make his way to the Pits.

"Getting hot now, Johnny boy," Tanya noted.

"Let me cash in and we can go get an ice cold beer."

"Sounds good. Just us two?"

"Solo para ti, corrina."

"What does that mean?" she asked.

"Only for you, Honey."

"Gracias," she replied, though it sounded like "Grassy Ass."

Tanya went to the Free Stuff section, a throwback to the Summer of Love and its free store, to see what treasures had been discarded. I cashed the load in. It didn't take long since the morning crowd had dissipated and I had everything sorted already.

"Will this fit you?" she asked, holding a green Bob Marley t-shirt up to my chest.

"Sure, you don't want it?"

"Nah, it suits you -- brown hair, brown eyes, green shirt, very treelike. Speaking of green, how much did we make?"

"Fourteen seventy-two."

"Great, we still have over fifteen left from yesterday."

"Let's go get that beer."

"Lead the way."

After buying the brew we strolled through the park to the picnic tables above the carousel. At least a hundred kids romped in the huge playground beyond.

Drinking peacefully while Tanya scanned the radio stations the beer was soon gone and I pulled the last can, now warm, from the backpack. This would be a tease for me but I thought of a way to get much more amusement from that twelve-ounce Bud.

"Ever shotgun a beer?" I asked.

"No. What's that?"

I placed the can flat on the table and poked a small hole on the bottom edge.

"Now what?" she asked intrigued by the process.

"Put your mouth over the hole and pop the top."

She considered my proposal. "It's warm"

"You'll never taste it," I declared.

She raised the can and pulled the pin. Gulping furiously, the beer was gone in a flash except for a little foam running down her chin.

Tanya turned to face me, her moon pie eyes the size of saucers. I thought for sure she would throw up. She grabbed her belly and opened her mouth.

"EERRRPPPP," she belched so loud that a family two tables over turned their heads.

"That's disgusting!" she wailed. "Errpp," a smaller burp snuck out.

"I thought you would like it."

"Don't I drink fast enough?"

"Fastest beer in the park," I answered, flipping the can into the trash.

"You're not saving it?"

"No place to carry it."

"Slacker."

We crossed Sharon Meadow to Hippie Hill. I slowed to watch Tanya for a moment, her jet black hair tucked beneath a bright blue bandana, her characteristic long coat, too warm in the brilliant sun, draped over her left arm. Noticing my gaze she walked back towards me with a sultry swaying gait. She flipped her head back, planting her right hand on her hip swinging freely from side to side. Tanya looped the coat around the back of my head.

"Come along, Big Boy," she pouted in her best Mae West.

As was nearly always the case on a beautiful Sunday afternoon, the park was buzzing with activity. The air surrounding Hippie Hill was filled with the pungent aroma of marijuana.

"Want to come back for the drum circle?" Tanya asked.

79

"Sure, what time?"

"Two or three, I'd like to see it."

"Sounds like fun."

Climbing Stanyan Street from John F. Kennedy Drive to the Pits I stopped to collect my breath and gaze up at the neon signs atop St Mary's.

A shiver ran down my spine as I thought back to a day, years before, when I helped install them. New to California and anxious to prove I could do the job, I dangled from the parapet, my harness and safety lines the only things preventing a nine-story fall to the parking lot below.

I pointed to the tower one hundred fifty feet above. "Hey T, did you know I put those up there?" Truth be told, I only helped set the lights but I had spent two days swinging back and forth anchoring the scaffolding.

"No way, not way up there," was her firm reply.

"No, really, I worked for this company, DPI, they do all the maintenance for the hospital. I was working inside on another job when the foreman asked if I was good with heights. I wanted to get outside and I thought he was talking about a second or third floor roof so I said sure."

She looked like she wanted to believe this story but still wasn't quite sure.

I continued, "Next day I show up here and over I go."

"Were you scared?"

"Terrified, but I'd opened my mouth so I had to do it with a smile. In a few minutes you get used to it and its not too bad."

"You stop worrying about falling?"

"Yeah, you trust the ropes, but then you start fretting about dropping something and killing someone below," I explained.

"Did you?" she asked sharply.

"What? Drop something or kill somebody?"

"Either, both, you know what I mean," she replied exasperated.

"No, I tied off my tools but I had to be really careful handling hardware you know, nuts and bolts."

"Wow, you really worked way up there?" she asked seeking final confirmation.

"Swear to God," I stated quietly.

She stared as if she was trying to look inside me. "What happened to you?" she asked truly befuddled.

It was said without malice or condemnation, just a sincere query for which I had no answer. Tanya pulled me by the backpack's padded straps and kissed my forehead, a mother's kiss devoid of any passion, as if to say, I understand. At that moment, two emotions flooded my being. I felt fragile, and I knew that, at all costs, I must cast this feeling aside. The opportunity to purge my soul lay just over the hill at the Pits where reality ended in the mind-numbing spell of the booze.

* * *

"Johnny Jets! And Tanya too!!" shouted Pete Cummings, an inebriated smile spreading from ear to ear. "Where you two been hiding?" he asked.

"Here, there, everywhere…." replied Tanya. "You know the drill."

Pete switched to pirate mode, "Indeed I do, lassie, indeed I do."

"I need a drink, Pete, how 'bout you? I'm buyin'!"

"Capital idea, my good man."

I dropped the pack and produced two forty's, handed one to Pete and the other to Tanya.

"Is this the last one?" she asked.

"Yeah, I got a few bucks for more, just hang on to that last twenty," I pleaded more than ordered.

"Yes, yes you have my word."

"Where's Hoss?" I asked knowing how hard it would be to miss anyone his size.

"Went to the store with Steve the Cab Driver, they should be back soon," Pete answered.

Tanya and Pete moved off to watch a hotly contested horseshoe match between Kenny Nelson and Bob Pardini. I took the last gulp from Tanya's bottle and headed to the store for more.

Cindy's Liquor was the closest liquor store to the Pits; it was also the only one in San Francisco that I avoided like the plague. The owner was yet another Arab, perhaps

82

some long lost relative of Fuck You Frank's. I was beginning to think it was a requirement for a liquor license in the city. However, he despised me as much as Frank liked me. He claimed I had passed out drunk in his doorway and he had to call the police to have me removed. Now, I have passed out in doorways, but never his, and I've never been lucky enough to forget anything that involved the police. After allowing him a few days to calm down, I returned and attempted to straighten things out. He wouldn't hear a word of it and I left cursing him, his mother, and the camel he rode in on, but now I needed beer. A year had passed so I decided to give it a shot.

No one was at the register, but I could hear voices from behind the potato chip display. One would have thought I was robbing the joint, my heart raced, my palms sweated as I plucked two Olde English 800's from the freezer and stepped up to the counter. "One moment please," a voice called from the back in a thick Jordanian accent. I stood silently evaluating my chances. I had lost maybe twenty pounds, my long hair was now cut nearly military short, I was not drunk and I sported a recently grown goatee and mustache. The proprietor appeared and gave me a kind of "Do I know you?" look.

Four fifty," he said.

I dropped a ten on the counter, but not content to leave well enough alone I asked dryly, "Pardon me, sir, do you have any Grey Poupon?"

"What, what is that?"

"A mustard, sir, a delightful Dijon."

"No, no, grey mustard only yellow French's."

"Well, thank you in any case," I added with a nod.

"Have a good day," he said slowly placing the change on my outstretched palm, a puzzled expression frozen on his swarthy face.

"You also," I replied as I turned and sauntered out the door. Had my arms been longer I would have patted myself on the back all the way home.

Big Pat and Steve the Cab Driver had returned to the pit by the time I arrived, Kenny Nelson had edged Bob Pardini in a nail biter with a last shot leaner and Tanya sat talking with Joy, while Lizard her Rhodesian Ridgeback ran up and down a sloping tree as was his habit.

Joy was tall with reddish blonde hair parted down the middle and blown back. Her shapely legs were crossed as she sat on the bench in a tight denim skirt with a slit up one side. A green top, baggy but bare at the shoulders, teased that the rest was just as enticing -- definitely a snappy little dish, quite easy on the eyes. I dropped the pack and pulled out one of the beers.

Tanya had returned to regulating my intake with the fish pucker method.

"What's that all about?" asked a bewildered Joy.

"Oh, he drinks too fast," answered Tanya.

"Really."

"Not too much, just too fast. I'm afraid I'll never get any."

"Keep the whole bottle," suggested Joy.

"Usually he buys, I'd feel bad."

"Enough ladies," I said and joined Pat and Steve on the high curb that ran the length of the Pits.

84

As I walked away I heard Joy say, "Well that was rude, we weren't even talking to him."

The boys shared a few hits of weed from Pat's small stone pipe. I deferred when it was passed to me.

Pat took a long pull, held it in for a minute, then released, asking, "Don't smoke, Johnny?" his face disappearing behind the intoxicating cloud.

"No, I get too stupid if I smoke that shit."

"Really, not even a little?" asked Steve.

"Not often, a hit here and there, usually when I'm drinking, and I forget how dumb it makes me."

We sat in the sun as bottles and the occasional pipe passed from hand to grimy hand. Conversations became shouting matches, the volume climbing to jet engine levels. Tanya approached and repeated her earlier suggestion about joining the drum circle. We said a few good-byes, promising to return though no one really cared if we did or didn't. Joy tagged along looking for some pot.

A short, rather enjoyable, downhill walk brought us from the Pits to Hippie Hill, to join the spectacle that is the Drum Circle.

An amazing sight, the Circle is a remnant of the Summer of Love that seized San Francisco forty years before -- pure Haight Ashbury, flower power madness. Bongos and congas of all shapes and sizes appear magically on weekend afternoons, pounded by drummers whose tastes and abilities varied to match their brilliant bandanas.

Stormtrooper boots flanked by hundred dollar Nikes tapped in time to the vicious beat. Leather and Levis stretched tight over gyrating asses, breasts bounced and swayed beneath soft cotton or linen, striated muscle glazed in sweat fell from flannel ripped and torn. Backs and arms twisted, etched with black barbed wire, thorny roses and menacing daggers. T-shirts strained to confine massive bellies filled with and created by oceans of pisswater beer. Onyx and jade, silver and topaz sparkled and flashed from wrists, navels, fingers and ears. Blackened eyes, their whites streaked with crimson blood vessels ruptured by brawling and whiskey hid behind mirrored sunglasses. All of it wiggled or watched from the lush green grass on Hippie Hill.

We dropped to the ground above three-dozen warriors pounding their skins with glorious glee, as the sweet skunky smell of the ganja wafted on the breeze. We entered a state of wild abandon, chugging huge gulps of wine from a cardboard box, swilling it carelessly over our chins and down the front of crusty shirts. Tanya swung her head from side to side as her hair flying from her neck in a centrifugal rage. The primal thumping built to a crescendo, then the drummers lost their way, crashing in percussive chaos as Tanya's head fell like a stone into my lap.

"Now I need a cigarette," she said as my brain pulsed. I pinched the sides of her nose and poured some wine into her mouth. Tanya coiled a hand behind my neck and brought my mouth to hers, spitting the wine back as our tongues entwined.

The circle wound down, musicians splintering away. We climbed back to the Pits with the palpitating rhythm still hammering on our brains.

The fog came hard and heavy that evening so we opted to stay on the hill above the Pits where it was a little warmer. Tanya spoke softly as the dew dripped from the upturned leaves around us.

"What day is it?" she asked.

"It's Sunday, almost Monday," I answered. "I can recycle here tomorrow and turn in at Kezar. LaPlaya is closed."

"What's the date?"

"The twenty-third," I answered, a rare occurrence that I actually knew.

"Well, I get a check on the twenty-sixth from GA. We can go downtown to pick it up."

"Really? That's Wednesday," I added, counting the days in my head.

"Yep 9:00 a.m., I have my final intake interview, I can't be late. I should have a check by noon." She smiled, "Some real money, Johnny Boy. You can take a day or two off."

"That would be great. I can sign up too. I have to actually or they cut off my stamps."

We slept curled tightly in each other's arms, our temporary camp not as cozy as home but for a day or two it worked fine.

I awoke at sun up and descended the hill to the Pits. Big Pat reclined on one of the green wooden benches wearing the prized Raider sweatshirt I had given him a day earlier. He passed me a half full fifth of Jack Daniels and I gladly took a pull to keep my buzz going.

"Where you off to this morning, Johnny Boy?" Pat asked, his distracted stare falling on the bourbon, golden in the early sun.

"Got to go do some recycling. We're pretty close to broke," I replied nonchalantly.

"Can I tag along? Got nothing else to do."

"Sure," I answered, delighted at the prospect of company and Jack Daniels. "I'll get a beer at Cala -- we need a chaser."

"Lead the way," said Hoss as he rose from the bench, his massive frame creaking and cracking.

We headed out into the surrounding neighborhood. Pat told me someone named Eddie came by the Pits after Tanya and I left, with cocaine. A good part of the group partook of the free lines he offered with many of them buying more. Most had crashed but Pat was still going strong.

The morning proved profitable and I cashed in at Kezar with just under thirty bucks. I noticed Pat standing near the free stuff and debated how much of the take to share with him. Suddenly his head fell back and he collapsed, smashing the back of his head against the base of a thirty-yard dumpster. I ran to his side as his body began to shake violently, foam spewing from his mouth.

"He's having a seizure!!" shouted Greg, one of the HANC yard employees, as he ran by me screaming to the booth to call 911.

I pulled Pat up by the collar of the Raiders shirt, wrapping my arms in a bear hug around his neck to keep him from smashing his head over and over on the asphalt. His blood was everywhere. I closed my eyes and held on until the spasms subsided. After what seemed like hours, a gloved hand touched my shoulder. I turned to see a paramedic on one knee beside me.

"We can take it from here," he said gently, sliding a restraint below Pat's head as a gurney was lowered from the ambulance behind us.

I gave the paramedics the small amount of Pat's background information I knew, washed his blood off me with a garden hose, and grabbed a shirt and shorts from the free stuff. Neither fit. As the ambulance carted my buddy off, I stuffed the thirty-dollar wad into my new baggy shorts, relieved that Pat was alive, in good hands, and that I didn't have to share the loot.

Returning to the Pits I spread the word about Pat. The mood was somber early on but even the near death of one of the gang could not keep things down for long. Fears and prayers gave way to song like we were at an Irish wake. As night descended, Pete Cummings sang, for the first of many times, in his raspy Celtic tone, Ed McCurdy's antiwar classic, "Last Night I Had the Strangest Dream," and for the first of many times I choked back tears.

* * *

One morning I was rummaging through a recycling bin at Fulton and 8th Avenue when a voice called out to me. "Hey buddy, want some more bottles?" a man shouted from across the street.

"Sure," I answered, pushing the buggy towards his open garage.

He pointed to three cases of empty Budweiser bottles stacked on the concrete floor. As I was loading them he dragged an old wooden foot locker from the rear of the garage.

"Take these too," he said, opening the lid to reveal about twenty booze bottles.

I started to explain that they wouldn't pay me for liquor bottles but I would donate them and bring the box back. He smiled, saying, "Dude, they're full. I joined AA four months ago; these things are calling me every night."

My face lit up like a kid on Christmas morning as I bent down to see all the unbroken seals and real corks in the bottles.

"Thanks, guy, I mean, really, thanks a lot."

I slid the foot locker on to the small shelf intended for heavy items at the bottom of the cart, gave his hand one last shake and made for the recycling center a block away.

I cashed out with about fifteen dollars and headed back to Fulton Street to grab the bus.

I rode out to 43rd Avenue and dragged the crate back to camp. I wanted to wait until dark but the booze was too valuable to stash. I carried the locker a few yards at a time, resting to scan my surroundings and check my back trail. After half an hour I stood safely in front of the tent.

I opened the lid of the locker and fished the bottles out one by one: two fifths of Absolut, Jack Daniels, Tanqueray, Smirnoff and Jose Cuervo, a dozen bottles of wine and the crown jewel, a fifth of The Macallan single-malt Scotch. I could not believe this day.

I packed the booze away and hid it in the tent under a pile of blankets and dirty clothes. I went to the Chinese noodle house opposite Block Head Joe's, got some dinner and rushed back to my treasure. That night it was a relief to have the camp to myself as Tanya, and Sam never returned. I drank until I passed out, one hand on the prized crate beneath a pile of dirty laundry.

The next morning, after a fitful night's sleep, I stood in the tent wondering why I was unable to get any real rest. It dawned on me that I could not keep all the booze. The bounty had placed a burden on me with which I was not used to dealing with.

Normally I worried about how to get booze. Now I worried about how to keep what I had. This proved far more insidious. I packed up a pair of paper shopping bags with two-thirds of the bottles, keeping one vodka, half the wine and, of course, the exquisite single malt.

A bag in each hand, I walked through the woods taking great care not to rattle the bottles together and break one. Twenty minutes later I arrived at Danny's. For security's sake I waited across the street until I was sure the store was empty. When all was clear I walked in the door.

"Hello, my friend," Danny said smiling, knowing I had come to pay the tab. "What's in the bag?"

"Something you might like," I replied, lifting the bags to the counter, the clink of the glass giving the contents away.

"Where did you get these?" Danny asked, inspecting each bottle and checking the seal.

"Someone gave them to me, a guy who quit drinking over on 8th Avenue said he couldn't keep them in the house anymore."

"Not stolen are they?" he asked testing my eyes.

"No, I was digging through the trash cans and he called me over and asked if I wanted them. I can't drink all this, thought maybe I could trade them with you for some credit."

Danny went to his adding machine and rang up the numbers. "Looks like $300.00. I can give you half."

"Half plus two beers and my tab," I countered.

"How much is the tab?" he asked.

"I know its less than twenty -- eighteen and change I think."

"You have a deal. Go get two beers," Danny said, pulling a ledger from behind the register.

On one page was my tab which he crossed out with a big red X; on the opposite page, beside my name, he wrote, "Credit $150.00," in black marker. "When you come in, we write down what you get and you sign the page."

"Thanks Danny, now I won't always owe you."

"You always pay, that is what is important; now go, I have a business to run."

I hit the street giddy from the transaction -- two frosty cold fortys, more booze back at camp and $150.00 in the Bank of Danny.

The day was going as brilliantly as the sun shining above. I moved west along Judah then turned north to avoid the 7-11 where my cronies lay in wait for anyone with alcohol. I always shared with people I liked and usually with those I didn't, but today I didn't need the baggage sure to follow an open bottle.

Just before I crossed Lincoln, I saw a queen-sized mattress and box spring propped against a garage door, next to an old throw rug. Scotch-taped to the side of the box spring, a single sheet of loose-leaf paper announced in scratchy ball point, "Free." I hoisted the heavy mattress to my shoulder and with the bag of beer dangling below, carried it off to stash at the edge of the park. I returned and repeated the process with the box spring, making a third trip for the rug.

"Need some chairs?" a woman's voice queried.

"What?" I asked, turning to see a young woman with a baby girl about a year old, fast asleep, balanced on her hip.

"We have a table and some wicker chairs, they go with the rug," she added.

"I'm sorry, I thought you were throwing this away," I said.

"We were hoping someone could use it. Still in good shape, the table and chairs are in the garage. I'll open it up."

She disappeared into the house; after a minute or two the garage door buzzed and began to rise. She reappeared, minus the tot, from a white metal door at the rear.

"Take it all," she offered. "Lamps too if you want."

"Thanks so much, but I don't really need lamps ... uh?"

"Julie," she said. "Did you just move in?"

"Yes, Julie, down Lincoln a little towards the beach. I'm John, nice to meet you," I answered as I reached out to shake her dainty hand.

"Well I've got to get back to the baby. Just push that button when you're done."

"Thanks again,' I added.

Hauling the table and chairs to the edge of the park was the easy part. My camp was clear on the other side. I couldn't transport the load through the park during daylight or my site would no longer be secret. After dark the chore would be nightmarish, navigating the trails, unable to see obstacles. I got an idea, an inkling of a plan, so I grabbed the beers, left the pile, and headed to the beach.

On these hot summer days, along the south end of the beach parking lot, many people stopped in to stare at the waves, and a lot of them have pickup trucks. I strolled along the concrete sidewalk, ducking down to the sand for swigs of brew. Rising up from one such foray, a possible solution appeared before me in the form of a red 1988 Chevy pickup backed into the curb. Two young surfer dudes sat on the tailgate scanning the waves. I walked up.

"You guys want to make a few bucks?"

"Sure, what you got in mind?" the taller guy asked.

94

"I need to move a little furniture from there," I pointed towards Lincoln, "to the other side of the park and I don't have a car."

"Is it a lot of stuff?" the stockier one queried.

"No, I was going to try and carry it. It's just one load in a truck."

"Any steps? he continued.

"Nope, curb to curb, won't take more than a half an hour," I replied.

"How much?" the tall guy asked.

"Twenty bucks, that's all I have."

They looked at each other and shrugged. The tall guy spoke, "What the hell, that's a few drinks."

"What do you guys drink?" I asked setting the snare.

"Usually beer, sometimes vodka and seven," he answered.

"You like Absolut?" I sprung the trap.

The two heads snapped to attention. "Absolutely!" they shouted in unison.

"I got a fifth for you if you help me out."

"A fifth of Absolut for a few minutes work?" asked the tall one.

"That's it," I said.

"I'm Dean," said the stocky guy. "This here's Neil. Lead the way."

"I'm Johnny, Johnny Jets, real pleased to meet you."

They got in the cab, I flipped up the tailgate and clambered into the bed.

"Where's the stuff, Johnny?" Dean asked.

"Around that corner, one block up," I said.

Neil fired up the truck, its loud pipes boomed. I took an immediate liking to these boys. They were just down from Seattle for the first time. They looked like a cross between Patrick Swayze and Keanu Reeves in *Point Break* and Bert and Ernie. We shot from the parking space and lit out onto the Great Highway, slicing deftly across three lanes of traffic into a tire squealing left turn. I slid across the truck bed grabbing at the side rail to keep from tumbling out. Neil punched the gas. I banged on the rear window and pointed at the load on the opposite side of the street. Dean nodded his head, gave me a thumbs up, and punched Neil on the shoulder. The truck wheeled into a high "G" U-turn. I bounced off the side rail again. We dodged a Volvo and skidded to the curb. I leapt from the truck, the boys sprung from the cab behind me.

"That's all of it Johnny? What's it doing here in the park?" Dean asked.

"I live here, well not right here, but in the park, on the other side," I explained.

"In the park?" Dean repeated.

"Yeah, it's a long story."

"Far out," said Neil.

We loaded the truck in minutes. "Where to?" asked Neil.

"The north side, Fulton and 43rd stop at Safeway and I'll get you a mixer."

We piled into the cab, this time with me in the center of the front seat, thankful to be out of danger, or at least the danger of falling out of the bed. Neil drove like a bank robber, hitting almost sixty on the half-mile stretch along the beach. Stomping the brakes he slid out the rear on the right turn onto Fulton. Safeway loomed to the left, a hard left, right combination. We swung in and nosed up to the door.

"Executive parking," I commented as Dean stepped out to let me slide by.

I returned to the truck with a two-liter 7-Up and three paper cups with ice from the soda fountain. The entire cost of the move came to less than four dollars plus the found bottle. We roared off, barely getting moving before it was time for the brakes again. Dean stepped out I slid across the shiny vinyl seat to jump from the cab.

"I'll be back in a few minutes," I announced, sliding the mattress off the truck. They stared warily, so I dropped my pack as a gesture of good faith.

The mattress weighed a ton but I moved rapidly towards the camp, dropping it on its edge to drag it through the thorns to the tent. I slipped inside emerging seconds later with the premium vodka. Back at the truck Dean and Neil had unloaded the rest of the stuff by the time I shot from the brush, Absolut in hand. I passed the bottle to a beaming Neil.

"Thanks guys," I puffed, bent over, my hands gripping the tops of my knees.

"Damn, Johnny, sure am glad we ran into you," said Dean admiring the label. "Think I'm gonna play bartender."

"Cups are in the front seat," I told him.

He reached into the cab, spun the key and the radio popped to life. While Dean mixed the drinks, I shouldered the box spring and set off on my second run, anxious to get things done and minimize unwanted attention. I returned to find the boys sitting on the wicker chairs, drinks on the table. Needing a rest, I picked mine up and took a pull. It reminded me of Black Joe's nightcap and Tanya. Setting the drink in the truck bed I hopped up on the tailgate.

"You really live in the woods, John?" Dean probed.

"Yeah, off and on, for the last five years -- lately more on than off," I acknowledged.

"Far out," chimed Neil.

"What about the off time?" Dean continued prodding.

"Sometimes get a room for a few weeks, most times jail," I admitted frankly.

"Ouch, that's gotta hurt," he grimaced.

"Not as much as you might think. When it's raining for a week, three hots and a cot isn't too bad."

"All this stuff fits in your camp?" Dean asked.

"Yeah, if I set it up right."

"Far out," said Neil, "Can we see it?"

"I could show you, but then I'd have to kill you," I replied smiling.

"We understand," said Dean as we shared the laugh.

A few more pulls, the friendly conversation, and Brooks and Dunne crooning "My Maria," conspired to relax me into dropping my guard. I was dog-tired and there was still work to be done.

"You guys really want to see my camp?" I asked.

"Sure," said Dean.

"Far out," echoed Neil.

"Grab your chairs and follow me," I said standing to down the last of my hooch.

We scurried up and over the hill across the meadow and along the twisting trail to the thorns.

"How much further?" Dean questioned.

"We're here," I answered.

"Where?" asked Neil. "I can't see it."

"That's the idea," I reminded them. "Follow me, but watch your eyes."

I clasped the table in both hands and bulldozed through to the pines. Their mouths fell open as they took in the camp in the fading light, their awestruck expressions filling me with pride.

"Far out," Neil uttered again.

"Jesus, Johnny this is sweet. How long did all this take?" asked Dean.

"It took a while, but the stuff today, with you guys, really finishes it off."

"This is something else. You got a girl too?" pryed Neil, seeing Tanya's things in the tent.

"I think so, hope so. I guess time will tell," I affirmed. "Come on, let's get back before someone steals my rug."

"No one would do that," Neil answered.

"How do you think I got it?" I winked to Dean.

"Far out," Neil murmured behind me.

We slipped through the trees and arrived at the Chevy.

"Another round, Johnny?" asked Dean.

"No, you guys keep the hard stuff, I'm good with beer."

They bounced into the cab and Neil fired the motor up. Dean handed my pack out the window and I pulled out the forty.

"You guys keep an eye out for me, I'm always at the beach."

"We will, Johnny. It has been a blast," said Dean, shaking of my hand.

"Far out," said Neil for the last time with a wave. He dropped the pickup in gear and they roared, tires squealing, into the night never to be seen again.

Walking back to camp my solitude began to engulf me, like the evening mist enveloping the jagged shore beneath the Cliff House. A night to gather my thoughts was one thing, but being out here alone was no fun at all. I returned to camp and threw myself into decorating to combat the building loneliness.

I set the boxspring and mattress to the right of the tent, finishing it off with a pile of blankets. It fit nicely beneath the awning, in the niche between the side of the tent and the heavy border of thorns. I rolled out the rug, added the table and chairs, hoping to finish my project before going for something to eat, but darkness and hunger got the best of me, so I crept down the hill to Safeway.

While gathering up a fried chicken, some Cheetos and, of course, more beer, I passed the housewares aisle. Amid the collection of dustpans and cookware was a section containing candles of all types.

"Ah, what the hell!" I groused to myself, and selected a hefty, white, rectangular number and two elegant, green tapers better suited for a table set with china and crystal than wicker and paper cups. I paid the cashier, asking for a book of matches in case my lighter was nowhere to be found.

Making my way back up the hill I slipped into camp unseen and collapsed in one of the wicker chairs to devour the chicken and Cheetos. In between hideously large chunks of meat and handfuls of processed cheese-flavored snack puffs, I slid the tapers into the necks of two empty Corona bottles, lighting them to allow rivulets of wax to roll down their sides over the cool glass, anchoring and ornamenting the two to create weighted candlesticks. I placed the stout, square candle between them in the center of the table, retreating slightly to admire my handiwork -- the effect was impressive, hypnotic, soporific.

I retrieved a bottle of The Macallan single malt scotch from the locker, popped the cork and took a long slow draw savoring the distinctive flavor -- definitely an acquired taste -- a blend of black eyes, failed marriages, fleeting youth, and heaven.

After months of sleeping on the hard ground, the lure of the bed proved too much for me. I returned the single malt to the safety of the wooden locker, shed my shirt and shoes, then crawled wearily between the blankets. The warmth and opulence of my new sleeping quarters drove me swiftly into oblivion.

*   *   *

Hours later a cry pierced the night. I opened my eyes to escape my dream.

"John, where are you?"

I shook my head to clear the cobwebs and disbelief.

"JOHN!!! I know you're out here. Come find me!" The volume grew.

I booted up and grabbed the flashlight. Tracking her was easy, I just followed the booming cries. I noticed movement in the bushes off to my right. Lifting the flashlight I froze her in the beam.

"Johnny Jets, that better be you," she turned, shielding her eyes.

I walked over and kissed her.

"Where'd you go?" Tanya asked. "I was looking for you."

"Just came back here, made some money, and finished fixing up the camp," I replied.

She had not done too badly -- we were less than fifty yards from the thorns.

As we arrived beneath the pines I instructed, "Cover your eyes."

Tanya complied. I went to the table and lit the three candles.

"Open them, take a look."

She dropped her hands and gasped at the sight of our new home.

103

"John this isn't a campsite, it's a hotel room in the woods!"

"So you like it?" I fished.

"Like it? I can't believe it!" she laughed, jumping high in the air, and bouncing on the bed. "Where did you get all this, I mean, where did it come from? How did you get it here?"

I lay next to her in the night. I told her of Julie, and her baby, and the furniture. Of recycling, and meeting Dean and Neil, of the constant "Far Outs," and the warp speed moving job financed by top shelf vodka given to me by a now reformed boozer at 8th and Cabrillo. I told her of the foot locker, paying Danny's tab, and getting the credit. She listened with rapt attention as the flickering candle flame danced on the wrinkled underside of the tarp.

"You got a whole box full of booze?" she asked.

"Mostly wine left now," I snickered. "I had bills to pay."

"Well, I still have some money, but the stores are closed, and I would love some wine."

"Wine, coming right up," I said heading to the foot locker inside the tent. "cabernet sauvignon ok ?"

"Sounds good, we need cups," she replied.

"One thing at a time, woman, I'm just a single man!" I hooted in a Scottish brogue.

"No, you foolish man! I have them in me satchel," Tanya hooted back. She unzipped her duffle to produce two cups.

After pouring the wine I sat back in a chair, Tanya picked hers up and sat down in my lap.

She gave me a quick kiss and let out a yawn. 'I'm really tired, how about hitting the hay Johnny Boy?"

"You're the one who woke me," I teased.

We slipped into the bed. Snuggling closely, she ground into me.

"A bed," she chuckled softly, "in the woods no less, you are unbelievable."

"Go to sleep," I said.

"You too." Intent on getting the last word she added, "You know I might just keep you."

*   *   *

Sammy reappeared later in the week but he was not alone. Beside him, a pack on his back, carrying a large stack of blankets, stood big Pat, eyes still blackened but looking much better than a few days before. "Got room for one more?" Pat asked tentatively.

"I could clear a spot in the garage," I kidded.

"Think Tanya will mind?" Sam asked.

"I'll go find out," I said. Walking back towards the tent, I whispered in the door, "Tanya, Big Pat needs a place to stay. Do you mind if he sleeps down by Sam?"

"Is Sammy back?" she asked, peering out from the tent. "Oh yes, and look what followed him home. Are we starting Boys Town now, John?"

"Hey Tanya," Sam said with a sheepish wave.

"And what have we here?" she chided Pat.

"I keep biting my tongue when I'm sleeping, like little seizures," Pat explained. "Just don't want to be alone now."

"Don't sweat it, we'll have some fun," was all she said and that's exactly what we did.

Pat moved in alongside Sammy at the front of the camp. This was fine with me. There is always strength in numbers and I now had two ferocious guard dogs protecting the gates of our camp.

We fell into a happy coexistence, each of us contributing something to the camp, all of us benefitting from the relationship.

I would leave early each morning to recycle, returning home with coffee and beer. Tanya and I would meet at the recycling center to head downtown to keep our appointments with the welfare department. We'd do this for a month or two then screw up and have to start the entire process over again. The account at the Bank of Danny rose and fell but never eclipsed its initial deposit of $150.00. Tanya took to decorating the camp, picking up all kinds of posters and macabre little statues. She placed a line of voodoo heads on arrows I retrieved from the archery range to protect the camp, positioning them along the path through the thorns to ward off evil spirits and unwanted strangers.

Pat and Sammy sometimes came with me to recycle but most times went out to drum up some cash on their own. We wanted for nothing. We always had a little more money, or a little more booze, or something we could sell to get it.

Pat possessed the uncanny ability to walk through a store, buy a one dollar beer and then pull a fifth of whatever was nearest the door from beneath his shirt as soon as we were safe in the woods. He was so good at it that even when I watched closely, nine out of ten times, I didn't see him do it.

Sam always had some hustle going on, from selling high-end clothes found in curbside donations to the Buffalo Exchange, a used clothing boutique on Haight Street, to helping a few elderly friends with chores and errands.

The growing permanency of the camp became evident from Pat's stack of bicycles, Tanya's ornaments and piles of clothes, and Sammy's portable black and white television set. The set ate batteries at a staggering rate but I found a discarded car battery that I charged once a week at the gas station for five bucks. This low cost electricity allowed us to stop swiping batteries from stores around the Bay. We spent the last few weeks of October watching the 100th World Series as the Florida Marlins defeated the New York Yankees four games to two.

* * *

Out by the beach we were part of the local crew that included Rif Raff and Kelly, two characters whose grungy, disheveled appearances served them well. These two older lunatics always had a bottle, usually a big one, they loved to share. A born comedian, Rif Raff patrolled the beach parking lot raising the bar for beggars everywhere with his quick-witted comments and slapstick. Kelly was his straight man, his Bud Abbott, the two were inseparable.

One rainy Tuesday morning, the kind where the steady winds turn the droplets into needles stinging any exposed skin, Sammy, Tanya and I walked along Fulton to the bus stop at Safeway. A fire truck and ambulance blocked the eastbound lanes. We approached cautiously to find a sobbing Rif Raff huddled on the bench, a bright yellow body bag behind him in the grass on the hill.

The fireman turned and asked, "Guess you guys know him." Rif Raff lifted his dirty face, eyes puffy from crying.

We all nodded, mumbling his nickname, the only one we knew.

"How about his buddy?" he asked pointing to the yellow bag.

"Kelly?" Sammy wondered aloud. "He in the bag?"

"Maybe you can tell me."

Sammy walked to the rear of the stop, crouching low over the bag as the fireman drew down the zipper. I turned my head away as Tanya pushed her face into my shoulder.

109

"Yeah that's him," Sam said. "Kelly Harper."

"That's what the ID says too," the fireman confirmed.

A wave of his hand signaled that Kelly be lifted into the waiting ambulance. By the side of the bench was a Safeway bag with an open half-gallon of Popov Vodka, a few dollar bills visible through the thin plastic clinging to the bottle in the driving mist.

Rif Raff stood and picked up the sack. "He would have wanted me to have this," he said to the astonished fire fighter, who looked to us for confirmation.

"Probably," I answered.

Rif Raff hunched off down the path to towards the Beach Chalet to mourn the death of his best friend by drinking the same vodka that had probably killed him.

Kelly was the first I saw die but far from the last. A thousand thoughts clashed in my head. Maybe he had health issues? Or had bad luck? But I was strong as an ox. My internal debate raged – Kelly's fate could not possibly be, yet most certainly was, what lay in store for me. As the trucks disappeared over the hill to the east my sadness barely eclipsed my sense of foreboding. A friend, a really good guy, had dropped dead at the bus stop and no one even cared. I was a good guy too.

* * *

Pat and Sammy began hanging out at the Pits more. I steered clear of that area because of some missed court dates that resulted in warrants being issued. I would be locked up if the police stopped me. The Haight was always a hot bed of police activity so I stayed by the beach where it was quieter, safer.

My discretion stemmed from my arrest three years earlier for domestic violence when I allowed a girl named Bridget to stay in my hotel room for a few nights during one of my "getting my life together" periods. I had sobered up enough to get some work at the recycling centers and managed to get some help from the welfare office to get a room.

We argued and I told her to, "Get the fuck out."

She stood and screamed, "You fuck with me and I'm gonna wreck your life."

She stormed off. I slammed the door and twenty minutes later there were four police officers standing in the room.

Following her accusation that I had beaten her and held her prisoner in the room, I was arrested. A newcomer to the criminal justice system, I remained in jail for 166 days confident that the truth would eventually come to light. It never did, and at the behest of my third public defender, a typical dump truck lawyer who took on my case then threw me to the mercy of the court, in the end I took a plea.

Although I knew it was wrong, I was tired of fighting, tired of postponed hearings, and court dates with no end in sight. I learned the hard way that the scales of justice tip quickly in your favor when loaded with cash. I was a pauper and as the saying goes, "You can't fight City Hall."

The warrants were not going to go away. They preyed on my mind every minute of the day and night. Finally, in a rare moment of common sense, I said to Tanya, "Hey T, what would you think about me turning myself in?"

"Why would you do that?" she asked.

"I'm running out of options. Basically I'm down to two."

"What are they?"

"Turn myself in or cut and run," I said. "Running only makes sense short term, not much work for an unemployed, fleeing felon."

"That doesn't sound too good. Where would we go?" she pondered, chin perched on her palm.

"New Orleans, Florida, Seattle maybe, I still know a lot of people in New York," I summed up, thrilled at the plural "we" in her question.

"I don't know Johnny, without jobs, without money?"

"What about you?" I asked concerned for both her safety and the thought of never seeing her again.

"I can go to a shelter, I've been alone before," she answered with a kind of cheery resignation.

After evaluating the rewards and consequences, my decision practically made itself for me; I would turn myself in just after the first of the month, squirreling away my cash to better my stay behind bars. The time proved fleeting and my day of reckoning was swiftly upon us. Tanya packed away her things while I broke down the tent and packed as much as I could in the footlocker. During the last few days I had mapped out several good hiding places in the park, designating the best one for the locker so I crept out at darkness to salt it away.

We didn't say a word to Pat and Sam. They were spending more time at the Pits and the longer they thought we were still at our camp the better. We huddled atop the mattress beneath a few sparse blankets nursing a pint of brandy under the stars.

"Back where we started, Johnny boy," Tanya pointed out.

"Yeah, but it will be better. You deserve better."

"We deserve better." There was that word again.

In the morning I donned my pack, carrying a duffel bag of Tanya's clothes as well. She pulled the rest in a small, wheeled suitcase that nipped at her heels like a dog. We wove through the woods with Tanya cursing her case for continually toppling over as it bounced off tree roots along the trail.

Arriving at Danny's to secure some more booze, I checked the balance of the ledger. Just over fifty dollars remained -- my nest egg upon release. We jumped the N Judah and headed downtown. Tanya kept the brandy, I finished the beer. At 8th and Howard we kissed and said goodbye. She crossed the street to the Episcopal Sanctuary, I moved along Howard to 7th Street, turning south towards the jail. Along the way I bought a pint of Smirnoff and guzzled it before arriving at the door. I walked into the lobby and followed the arrows to the counter of the San Francisco County Sheriff's Department.

"I have to turn myself in," I explained to the redhead manning the desk.

"Excuse me?" she said.

"I missed a court date, so I have a warrant, so I have to turn myself in," I explained.

"Sarge!" she hollered over her shoulder pointing at a chair by the door.

I sat for a few minutes until a black man the size of a minivan appeared from behind the side door.

"What's up?" he asked politely.

The vodka was really kicking in now. "I have to turn myself in." I tried hard not to slur.

"You're drunk, go home and sleep it off," he ordered, fanning the air to clear my 100 proof breath.

"Correct, I am drunk," I continued. "But alas I do have to turn myself in."

"Why, you got a warrant?"

"Yep felony, no bail." That got his attention.

"You sure?" he asked, still trying to gauge my state of intoxication.

"Would I walk into a police station dead drunk if I wasn't?" I replied.

"I guess not. What else do you know about your case?"

"Department 13, Judge Kahn's courtroom," I recited. "Arrest date April 12th, 2002."

"Hold on," he replied, moving behind the counter to a computer.

The Sargent pecked at the keys as I repeated the information.

"No bail. Huh, you were right."

"Thank you," I acknowledged with a smugness only a drunk could muster.

The information revealed that since I was homeless I was considered a flight risk, hence the no bail warrant. I thought the city would be glad to see me go but my continued arrests pumped up the statistics allowing for more funding for law enforcement from the Federal Government. Once the officer determined I was not an escaped murderer the arrest went smoothly. I was soon dressed in orange, deposited in the holding cell just prior to the evening rush. I murmured a quick prayer and unceremoniously passed out.

*   *   *

Waking up a few hours later enclosed by yellowish beige walls with a tint of green. The colors, coupled with my churning stomach, remind me of bile and I fight hard to control the dry heaves. Curled into a corner, a roll of toilet paper crushed into a pillow beneath my head, I am one of the lucky ones. The less fortunate stand, or sit packed eight to a bench designed for five, or pace the cell out of frustration, boredom, or fear, stepping carefully to avoid the bodies strewn about the orange rubber floor.

Someone slams the hard, plastic receiver of the gleaming chrome wall phone into its cradle. The loud crack reverberates through the cell.

"Mother fucker!" a voice screams, heavy footfalls pounding across the room.

A tall, menacing black man grabs the vacated phone, cupping the mouthpiece, whispering until his rage gets the better of him. "What you mean you got no money?" he barks.

A moment goes by as his stare intensifies. "Better be some money on my books bitch, some real money or I'll beat your sorry ass, you feel me? I gets mine."

Beside him a young Mexican rattles on rapidly in his native tongue. He can't be more than twenty-five, but my guess is he's barely eighteen. From his staccato diatribe I make out a single, familiar word, "Mierda," Spanish for shit.

"Si," I think, straining to cobble together a single sentence. "Mucha mierda y soy en profundo."

"A lotta shit and I'm in deep."

Names are barked as they whisk us through the initial medical intake. My head pounds, I can feel the shakes begin. As a veteran of this process I seize the opportunity to get some pharmaceutical relief. I start doing push-ups, one after the other until I can do no more. My heart is racing when I hear the guard shout my name. I wipe the sweat from my hands and face with my shirt front and exit the fishbowl through the thick glass and steel doorway. With just the right amount of sweat beneath my shirt my skin turns cold and clammy in the chill of the air-conditioned hallway. An older woman, who reminds me of my aunt, waves me into the examination room. Wrapping a blood pressure cup around my left bicep, she inserts an electronic thermometer into my mouth. In an attempt to create some kind of medical profile she asks the usual questions. I mumble answers with the thermometer bouncing between my lips.

Her concern grows as she notes my unusually high pulse rate and blood pressure. She plucks out the thermometer.

"How are you feeling?" she asks placing her palm over my forehead.

"A little shaky," I respond with a hint of remorse.

"Do you drink?"

"Yeah, probably too much," I reply, the remorse growing.

"When was your last drink?" the nurse questions.

"Just before I got arrested."

"Ever have seizures?" She pops the million dollar question.

"Yes," I lie.

"Let me see your hands," she orders. I hold them out trembling sufficiently.

"Now your tongue," she adds. Faking the tongue wag is more difficult but I know the symptoms and practice makes perfect. A sad, reluctant smile parts the wrinkles of her chubby face.

"You know you really should quit."

"I know," I answer, casting my eyes downward, "I know," this time with a sigh.

She pats my arm, softly pronouncing the words I am hoping to hear, "I'll get you something to make you feel better."

The result of this virtuoso performance is four days' worth of Librium, a tranquilizer that eases the transition into sobriety and incarceration. I feel bad for having deceived this dedicated, caring public servant but quickly rationalize my need for the pills. All is fair in love and jail.

I spend the next three days as a resident of ICP, the Inmate Classification Pod, the purpose of which is to determine if you are well behaved enough to join the general population. This is accomplished by depriving you of any and all forms of distraction. No talking, no books, no TV, no working out -- nothing to do but sit and think about your crimes. The idea is to drive you crazy enough to do something stupid, which would result in a month-long stay. It is the first real taste of being locked up.

I sleep away the first two days and head to court on Day Three. My lawyer is not present at the appearance and the judge wants a probation report. Given the option of rescheduling or getting a new lawyer I choose the former. I really like my lawyer, Rosalyn. If she'd represented me from the start I probably wouldn't be in this mess. The court clerk reviews the calendar and I become a guest of the county for another three weeks.

Now that my stay in the jail would be close to a month, and I have been a model ICP prisoner, I am moved to the sixth floor of the old County Jail.

This is a real jail, built in the Forties, with long corridors flanked by rows and rows of heavy steel bars, with massive iron gates sliding on rollers or swinging on hinges as thick as my arm. The heavy clang of their locking mechanisms leave no doubt in my mind that I am here to stay. Some of the cells are arranged like dorms with rows of bunk beds. Others are small cells set up for one to six occupants -- these are generally reserved for more dangerous prisoners. I was sent to a dorm. Compared to the ICP, it is Disneyland. We have books, television, newspapers, showers, table games, a commissary, and movies on weekends. Compared to living outdoors for a few years, it was the Ritz and despite the threats and fights, the dangers were few and far between.

I read a book a day, and do hours of jailhouse calisthenics as a result of my renewed focus the three weeks pass by quickly. I appear before the court again, this time with Rosalyn Manson by my side.

"John, you will be out today, back on probation same terms as before," she informs me. "Any idea what you're going to do?"

"Not really. I have no place to go," I offer indifferently.

"What about your family? Could you go there?" she asks with genuine concern.

"I don't want to be a burden to them. I've been thinking about a program, maybe I'll go that route."

"That would also help your standing with the court," Rosalyn adds.

"I'll think about it."

They cut me loose at 10am, and I made a bee-line for the welfare office, leaving with a bag of tokens and appointments to get a check. I head for the bus stop on Mission. There's a young guy waiting for his ride at the stop. "Hey, would you need a token? I'm trying to sell one to raise a little cash," I ask.

"Sure, I could use two," he replied, handing me a five-dollar bill.

"I don't have change -- just got out of jail. I could give you two more."

"No man, no worries you need them more than I do."

Usually I would have delighted at the two-dollar gain, instead I felt a twinge of shame. A month sober had raised my self-esteem enough to allow me to see just how pathetic I had become. Asking him to buy the tokens was bad enough, but not being able to return his change demonstrated my utter lack of anything that resembled a life. I thanked him profusely, but did not board the bus when it stopped. I hated the feeling that I was a nothing and headed to Traveler's Liquors on 7th Street for the cure. I bought a forty-ounce and snuck down the alley to the parking lots.

I had not had a drink in a month and I knew I should not have one now but I was not ready to stop. I took a swig. It tasted dark and bitter, but I knew if I finished it things would begin to look up, the inadequacy would be gone, and so I drank on, waiting for the magic.

* * *

Grappling with my demons was a full time proposition even before I retired to the woods. Prior to losing my apartment I had a calculated approach to drinking. I built safety nets to minimize the consequences. I stashed money in the bank and under the bed for the rainy day I was about to create. I prepaid insurance, rent, and bills. On the surface this appeared to be responsible behavior, but in reality, my reserves enabled me to continue my self-annihilation while maintaining a façade of respectability. The funny thing is the only one I fooled with this behavior was me. I really believed that I was doing things the right way.

Tanya and I now stayed together as much out of necessity as anything else. It would be wonderful to think that love or destiny had joined us together, but at this point neither of us had anyplace else to go. Sometimes she would disappear for weeks and then pop back into my life. We both knew the end was near.

During one of my solitary periods I partied with Joe, Sammy, Charlie, and Black Mark. After finishing a fifth of Dewar's by myself I staggered into the night. The next morning I awoke to feel the shakes building. It was too early, and 7-11 and the liquor stores weren't open yet, so I headed to the beach hoping to score some booze before I was reduced to a vomiting, trembling mess.

The beach run produced two unopened cans of Bud, a half bottle of cheap red wine, and a few half empty beers, all of which I guzzled down as soon as I found them. The shakes in my hands eased and the band playing in my head quieted, but by the time I made it to the redemption center I felt the booze wearing off. Up for less than five hours, I had already fought through one bout of the shakes. If I could keep my head together for just a few more minutes I would have the cure and a plan.

The Salvation Army ran a detox downtown. If you had ten bucks you could usually get in right away. I would cash out, head down there, and be off the street, safe and sound.

If I got lucky they would send me to the hospital for a medical detox. If I was unlucky and had a seizure at least I would be in a bed and someone would call an ambulance. Most people don't realize there is no known medical treatment for the DT's. Grand mal seizures, heart attacks and stroke can occur, all of which can be fatal. Which is why drinking was always preferable to fighting the urge and getting sober. Your body craves the alcohol, your brain is telling you to get some more booze or you're going to have a seizure and die and you will do anything for that next drink.

I stood beside my buggy, wrapped up in a knockdown drag out battle with the obsession, cursing the recycling center workers who were already ten minutes late and nowhere to be seen. .

"Johnny Jets!" hooted the driver of a shiny, gold Chevy Astro van. "You're looking a bit rough, son."

"Don't I know it," I replied.

At the wheel was Terry Crumb, riding shotgun was Joe, another Irishman, both good friends from the Pits. Word on the streets was they'd been sober for the last six months.

"Need a drink?" Joe inquired casually.

123

"Oh yeah, I feel like I'm gonna die. Please, please tell me you have one?"

"No, but we can fix that. Hop in and we'll get you one at Block Head Joe's."

I was in the rear of the van in the blink of an eye, abandoning my load without a thought. We took off for the store, my relief in sight, the intolerable wait nearing an end. Joe slipped from the truck, returning with a pint of rotgut vodka and a forty dangling in a black plastic bag. He handed me the package, I opened the flask, took a polite swig and tried to hand it back.

"No, that's for you," Joe said. "Go on now and take a real belt, you need it."

The generous gulp that followed can only be described as glorious. I could feel the booze extinguish the fires in my mind like cascading water. I chased the cure with a leisurely swill of Olde English.

By the time we returned to the Safeway lot the center was open for business. Terry parked alongside my buggy and killed the engine. I had lost my spot in line but I cared little. The wait no longer mattered, I was normal again.

"What do you want to do, Johnny?" Terry asked. "You know you ain't gonna make it. What do you really want to do?"

I broke down then, rambling about everything, the frolicking fun times with Tanya, our quiet thoughtful nights and our deliriously decadent days. They listened quietly through it all, both veterans of recovery and relapse. They knew the inescapable anguish and the inevitable consequences of not being able to stop.

"So what is it you're planning then?" Joe asked gently.

"Once I cash this in, I'm heading to Salvation Army, then hopefully another program from there."

"You'll do it today?" Joe asked for confirmation.

"Soon as I get the ten bucks," I answered, buoyed by my rising blood alcohol content.

Joe pulled out his wallet and peeled off a ten. Still engulfed in foolish pride, I pushed the money away.

"I'll get my own as soon as I cash in," I declared.

Joe pushed the bill into my hand then folded my fingers tightly around it.

"Cash in and keep the money, just promise me *that* ten goes for the detox."

I pushed the money into my pocket. "You got it, Joe."

"Good man, now get your money and we'll take a ride."

We drove around for about an hour, our arrival at the Salvation Army coinciding with the demise of my bottles. Joe went to the door, spoke through a sliding window then returned to the truck with a shrug.

"They've no beds, Johnny, but they'll take you first thing Monday," he explained.

Disappointed, I wanted to run, find Tanya, and return to the drunken safety of the night. I had money and there was always more booze. I wouldn't even have to walk or hop the train, Terry and Joe would chauffeur me back to oblivion. Then a nagging sensation stirred through the numbness -- this might be my last shot at redemption. I blurted out the truth before self-deception took hold of

125

me again. "Joe, I won't do it," I confessed. "I won't be here Monday any more than I'll be standing on Mars."

"Why, John? You still have the money, you're all set."

"I didn't say I can't, I said I know I won't."

They understood. "They said Ozanam can take you today," Joe added, fully aware of what he suggested.

The Ozanam Detox Center was a drop-in center on Howard Street. If you hadn't been there in the past month, they would not turn you away. I knew the routine well and did not want to endure it again. I had used it as a place to crash on cold, rainy nights, as a way to shower and shave at moments of despair, as a mat for the night when I slipped out of jail in the wee hours. Crack smoke filled the toilets, booze was hidden in nearly all the packs. but they made good soup, and at least it was a chance, no matter how slim.

"Okay, I'll try it," I said. "But I'll need another pint."

The boys laughed knowingly. "That's a good man," Joe offered. "First to the liquor store then on to Ozanam."

My first day at Ozanam passed quickly as first days always do, the alcohol still in my system calming me, allowing me to try and rest. Day Two brought the shakes and anxiety mixed with depression that ballooned into suicidal dread. I shivered on my mat. Digging in my pockets I found a wad of crumpled bills. I counted eighteen dollars and stared at the door. Relief was barely a block away. I could leave right now, run for a bottle and a bed at Salvation Army come Monday. A thousand reasons urged me up and out the door. Pulling the thin blanket over my head I clung to the notion of staying sober one day at a time, one minute at a time. With all my remaining will power I struggled through the hours of misery, finally succumbing to sleep.

Day Three brought changes. I had passed the first cut and got moved upstairs to a bed and a shower. Staring into the mirror for the first time in weeks revealed the massive toll my lifestyle was taking on my body. Bloodshot eyes, teeth bloody after brushing, hands still shaking but a little less now, I cleaned up and ate. On the outside I looked a little better but on the inside I was still a mess, spending the remainder of the day in and out of bizarre dreams coupled with cold sweats but grateful to be here not enduring this alone, unaware that these were the essential first steps in reclaiming my life.

Day Four found me much improved. I could hold a glass of water at arm's length and not spill it. With the encouragement of the staff I began to make phone calls in search of a permanent solution. My stay at Ozanam was limited to seven days but I had money so the Salvation Army was still an option. If I was waiting for admission to a program, I could stay there for another three weeks.

Day Five, I got an interview with The Saint Anthony's Foundation. They had two six-month programs -- one in the city, another on their dairy farm to the north. Leaving Ozanam on a pass, I walked across Howard Street to the interview. Before I cleared the corner, a familiar shout rang from the alley, "Johnny Jets! Where have you been?" It was Indian Ed, another acquaintance from the tight knit community of the homeless, and an actual American Indian.

"I've been sober, Ed" I replied, careful to omit the fact that I'd been on the wagon barely five days.

"Good, good, you look great, come 'ere, look what I got."

Ed dug in his buggy, slowly, deliberately pulling a half-gallon of vodka by its long neck from the debris in the cart.

"That's great, Ed, but I just said I'm not drinking."

"What's the matter don't you feel good? Try some of this, it's the good stuff, it will really help," Ed badgered.

"Ed, I feel fine, peachy as a matter of fact."

"Good, so come on and have a belt," Ed repeated, oblivious to anything I said. He could not comprehend that I would ever not want a drink. I decided to attack the problem in terms he would understand.

"I would love to Ed, but I'm heading to probation."

Ed's brain finally clicked. "Oh, court, huh, you better not drink," he declared.

"You're right, maybe later," I agreed, waving goodbye.

The interview was short, two spots were open but unfortunately, I was number three. Returning to the detox, I spoke with the day nurse as she gave me the once over to be sure I hadn't been drinking. "Yeah, they'll do that to you, they want to make sure you're serious," she said.

The next day brought the same result -- I passed over again.

On my final day at Ozanam I left for the interview, hoping the third time really would be the charm. Again I was brushed aside, but I decided to take matters into my own hands. Instead of my usual polite goodbye, I rose and turned to Phil, the gentleman I had spoken with these past few days. Speaking clearly and calmly I stated my grievance.

"Look I don't know what, if any, game you're playing here but it took me months to drag my sorry ass into that detox. Today is my last day, so after I leave here it's back to the streets and you will probably never see me again. I want you to know you are playing with my fucking life here." After saying my piece I turned to the door.

"Wait a minute," Phil called after me. "You clean today?"

"Yes," I answered coolly.

"You're sure? We're gonna test you."

"Go ahead," I replied.

I was in the program that afternoon. After reporting for a physical, I took my pack with my one clean shirt to my new home, the Saint Anthony Foundation's Seton Hall on Guerrero Street.

As Sammy always told me, "The squeaky wheel gets the grease."

                              *   *   *

Mornings at Seton Hall meant six o'clock wakeups and early morning reflections, forty drunks and dope fiends gathered in circle to praise God and voice their concerns for the coming day, pressing issues like who forgot to fill the toilet paper dispenser in the third floor commode or why the newpapers' sports pages were being removed from the library. This, from men who a few days before thought discretely shitting in an alley constituted positive social behavior, and that newspapers were the equivalent of damask sheets.

Early on I would rather have been anywhere else. I longed for my tent beneath the pines, waking next to a smoldering bonfire at the break of day, and, of course, Tanya. Seton Hall was a no frills, stripped down, on-the-job recovery center in the heart of San Francisco's Tenderloin District. The court mandated the presence of many of the Hall's inhabitants, Hunger, poverty and despair mandated mine, and perhaps the higher power I was discovering and chose to call God also played a role.

We worked days serving food to hundreds of the homeless, nights we worked on ourselves. To a man we had all stood in the long line of the kitchen we now operated. The kitchen's daily spectacles served as a constant reminder of where we had been and if we were not extremely diligent, and more than a little lucky, where we would inevitably return.

The work continued with counseling each afternoon, AA meetings nearly every night and closing prayers at the end of the day.

The counseling was mainly a group affair, myself and five of my peers whose combined life experience included three suicide attempts, seven failed marriages, five fatherless children, at least two dozen squandered careers, and more than a half million dollars in revenue and property lost or spent in pursuit of our drugs of choice. As the elder statesman I alone accounted for a third of these totals.

I began to not hate the mandatory AA meetings, I liked just being a part of something, anything. I started listening to the messages of the speakers, the meaning beyond just their words. I had actually progressed to the point of getting a sponsor. I was becoming a recovering alcoholic instead of a practicing one.

Eventually I even grew to like the nightly prayers that I initially found hokey. I noticed that for the people who stuck around that they were a time to express gratitude for the many gifts we received each day. Even the smallest steps towards reclaiming our self-respect deserved to be recognized, and these nightly meditations provided a forum for acknowledging our good fortune. I liked going to sleep knowing that, for at least that day, I had done my best.

But change comes slowly, and as any alcoholic will tell you, change and slow are two very bad things. On one hand constantly rehashing all the screw-ups of my life seemed pointless, but on the other hand, for whatever reason, I was still sober. Every once in a while someone said something that stuck with me; I relied on those little bits of wisdom to keep me involved until the next one came along.

At the end of the first month we were given more freedom and, using the buddy system, we were allowed to travel about the City. My first stop, of course, was the Pits to show everyone how wonderful I had become.

The Pits had changed -- or maybe I had.

At first the changes weren't readily apparent because everyone was stoned. A group of researchers, maybe from UCSF, were studying the effects of medical marijuana on curbing other addictions. They supplied free pot to anyone who enlisted in the study. The regulars eagerly signed up, got as much pot as they could, smoked some, and unbeknownst to the scientists, sold the rest at the front of the park. They scrapped the experiment when half the Haight tried to volunteer and the investigators could not keep up with the demand.

During my second trip back, changes, ugly ones, began to rear their heads. An influx of dope and those who sold it had changed the complexion completely. The convivial, festive atmosphere of the Pits had been replaced by secretive bands of three or four people whispering among themselves, masking their devious, criminal acts in buzz words and street slang. The worst of these was Eddie the Peanut, an ex-con born with a nose for cash and no conscience. I had never met him although I had heard his name a few times before. He would routinely show up on check days with bags of heroin and crystal meth, selling the dope to anyone stupid enough or drunk enough to buy it.

I was walking up the hilly path from the Hayes Street entrance to the Pits, I noticed a body lying in the dirt beneath a bench where the trail split the trees. No shoes, no shirt, just muddy pants darkened by a large wet spot around the crotch. It turned out to be Terry, the same man who four months before had gotten me off the streets.

He was incoherent, disgraced, ostracized from his family, barely tolerated by his so-called friends. At this point they only put up with him for his money or rides in his van on the rare occasions he was sober enough to drive.

I pulled him from the ground and propped him on the bench. "Terry, Terry!" I said shaking him by the shoulders to force a response, any response. "Come on, wake up!" I shouted. His face barely acknowledged my presence let alone any sign of recognition.

"John?" he finally realized.

"Yeah man, why don't you come with me for tonight?" I plead. "You're filthy, let me take you down to Salvation Army, take a rest, get some sleep." I burned to get him some help, a start on repaying the favor I owed both him and Joe.

"No, no way, I'm fine," he slurred, unable to lift his chin from his chest.

"Terry, let me give you a hand. I'll even get the next bottle, just come with me now."

I had said the magic word, and suddenly he became animated. "I got a bottle, where's my fuckin' bottle?"

I tried to calm him down but the tirade continued, "Where's Pete? He's got my bottle. I just bought it. Where the hell is Pete?"

Terry staggered up the trail to find Pete and the precious missing bottle. I turned silently and walked back to the bus stop.

The few times we met over the next month Terry was wildly drunk, weeping on my shoulder that he loved me, that he was so proud of me, but he would not follow, he no longer cared. As it turned out that interaction at the bench was as close to a conversation as we got before he died.

Tommy Muldoon was the first of my cronies to die. Gregarious, about my age, he happened by the Pits' sporadically, staying for a day or two to have some fun then vanishing for the next few months. Tommy left one night on a beer run, bicycling to Frank's, the last store in the Haight to close. As he crossed Stanyan and Oak he clipped a curb and veered straight into the path of a MUNI bus, crushing and killing him a few hundred yards from the Pits.

Terry was next, his untimely end less violent but somehow far more heinous and cruel. He now lived in his van with Eddie the Peanut, and a girl named Corrine. Corrine, once quite pretty, now decimated by drugs and disease, with the lesions typical of full blown AIDS on her face and neck, clung to Eddie for her fix. Terry liked her despite the circumstances and allowed the pair to stay with him. One night, while the two of them were shooting some dope, Terry, too drunk to know better, produced forty dollars saying he wanted to join in.

Eddie, never one to turn down a quick buck, not only supplied the dope but cooked and administered the shot. Terry overdosed, the needle still in his neck. Eddie took the rest of his dope and money and ran off into the night. Corrine, to her credit, flagged down a car to call the police. By the time the ambulance arrived resuscitation was no longer an option. Terry Crumb, age forty-three, was dead.

Life in the streets is cheap. Terry's death made me realize that the tranquil green meadows of Golden Gate Park could be every bit as lethal as the cuts and alleys of the Tenderloin or Hunter's Point. Following the news of Terry's death the Pits no longer held any attraction for me. They seemed no better than a Skid Row alleyway full of dopers and hustlers seeking to get high and make a quick buck at the expense of anyone and everyone.

Seton Hall had served me well. As my time in the program wound down, my time sober continued adding up. I had even gotten some money from a lawsuit I had filed years before in New York and bought a small Nissan camper. Still, I had yet to face the acid test. No one had seen or heard from Tanya in months. I was moving away from my years in the Park but didn't want to go alone.

I was scheduled to finish the Seaton Hall program on July 2nd, job in hand, all my ducks in a row. We were already in the latter half of June so the smart money was betting on me to finish. As it turned out, the smart money had no idea how dumb I could be.

Exiting the Artists' and Writers' AA meeting at Waller Street I turned my cellphone back on as soon as I hit the street. There were six new messages, five from Tanya. She said she'd been in Marin working her own program, and a job as well; she was the proud owner of 1985 Chevy Blazer and wanted to see me. The fuse was lit but I still had a chance, another meeting might be the answer. Walking down Haight Street towards Walden and ARA House in search of an AA group, the final straw fell.

Big Pat stood in the doorway of Frank's. "Johnny, guess who I just saw looking for you?" Pat answered his own question, "Tanya."

135

"Yeah she called and left a message."

"You have a phone?" he asked.

At that moment I knew I was not going back. Tanya was here and I would find her. I left my number for her at North Beach then waited for her reappearance. Six months in a teetotaling malaise was long enough. As the AA gurus say I relapsed long before I took my next drink. None of that mattered now, Tanya was back and I was alive. In celebration, I bought Pat a beer but stayed sober on the off-chance that she was serious about her recovery. We lit out along Stanyan Street, climbing the steep hill to the Pits. Arriving at the benches, Pat drank his beer while I stuck with Diet Pepsi. A glint of light cut through the trees near the footpath.

"Cops?" asked Pat.

"At this time who knows," I answered. "Ditch the beer."

The silhouette of a vehicle slunk between the breaks in the bushes below. The headlights reared up, streaming skyward as the truck launched up and over the steep crest at the top of the path.

"Tanya!" chirped Pat.

"Yep, who else would be driving through the park at midnight."

The time had come, the moment for which I had been waiting. I stood and approached the truck, idling at the edge of the Pits. The passenger door flew open the dome light illuminating the interior and Tanya behind the wheel, looking better than she had in months.

"Mr. McHugh, you're looking well," she said.

"Likewise," I answered, adding, "Nice truck."

"Picked it up in Marin, hop in."

I stood at the crossroads. That car door was either the gateway to heaven or a portal straight to hell. I released my tenuous grip on common sense and climbed in. I leaned towards her cherubic face, we locked in a long embrace.

"Where to?" she whispered.

"Anywhere," I replied.

* * *

We spent the next few months searching for anywhere better than here. It was always just up ahead, around the next bend, or over the next hill, but all we found was nowhere.

Two impounded trucks and several thousand dollars later, we hitchhiked backed to Golden Gate Park. We were out of money and options. We had nowhere else to go.

My non-appearance warrants were up and running again.

One bright Sunday morning, I slipped down to the beach to enjoy a hard-earned forty. A police radio squawked behind me. Atop the dune stood a Federal Parks policeman, the mirror finish of his black patent leather shoes and the tip of his hat gleaming.

"What are you doing out here?" I asked.

"I wanted to ask you the very same thing," the cop replied.

"Sitting on the beach. Is that against the law?"

"Were you drinking?" he asked.

"Yes, I had one beer."

"One or twenty, it's still against the law," he responded.

"Is there really a problem with one beer, sir?" I pointed down the beach. "I passed at least ten people drinking on my way out here. See that couple with the kids, they're drinking wine --why not go talk to them?"

This was my first play, a confrontational style; it made the officer cringe. Maybe, I thought, I could convince him that he was really being an asshole.

"Officer, I came all the way down here so as not to disturb anyone, and not to be disturbed."

"Well it's not the beer so much as the glass," he answered.

"Sir, I recycle this beach every day. I stay alive by keeping it clean. I can show you bags of recycling I got this morning at dawn. Believe me, I am not going to leave a mess."

He rubbed his chin surveying the scene. Clearly there could be no complaint with the area near me.

"You have ID?"

Alas, the million dollar question.

Handing over my license I studied his face as he scrutinized the document, flipping it over and back in his fingers.

If he radioed my numbers in the warrant would definitely show, but there was still a chance I would get a break and walk off with a warning.

His hand reached to key the microphone pinned to his shoulder.

"Wait, hold on," I surrendered, blurting in despair, "I've got a warrant for missing a court date. If you run my name I'm going to jail."

"Why are you telling me this?" he asked.

"Because I don't want to go to jail," I answered.

It was a calculated risk. Had I said nothing and the warrant showed he would tell me that I should have said something before he radioed in. Now I hoped transparency might buy me some time.

"Listen I can get back on the court calendar Monday morning, I know I have the warrant and would like to handle it without being busted."

He dropped his hand for a moment to consider my request. After what seemed like an hour of hemming and hawing, he muttered, "Look, I'm just doing my job. I have to run you to be sure." He turned away and began speaking into his microphone.

"Sure of what?" I asked.

The report of my warrant came crackling back in standard police gibberish, a cryptic response ending with, "Copy?"

"10-4," the cop responded. Turning back to me, he said, "Looks like you were right."

"I would rather be free," I answered.

"Come on, I won't cuff you until you're at the car."

He was kind enough to let me gather my gear and lug it back across the dunes to the parking lot. I stashed it in the weeds by the curb on the off chance that I would be released quickly. In hindsight I should have fallen to the sand and forced him to drag me and my gear to his cruiser.

Retuning to jail brought no surprises. The methodical booking system shuffled me into my new home. I had not been hitting the booze as hard this time so I didn't need the Librium but I faked the whole process again anyway. A little chemical relaxation wouldn't hurt my slide back into captivity.

It was the weekend so I settled into my bunk and waited. Monday morning, I stood in a courtroom, my trusted attorney at my side. The powers that be offered to release me that afternoon in exchange for my signature, the reinstatement of my probation, and fifty-two weeks of anger management classes I had already failed to complete seven times. If I blew it again, I would get six months for the probation violation alone. After hearing these terms I asked for a few minutes to speak with Rosalyn and was returned to the holding cell to wait for her.

Seated numbly on the concrete shelf that served as a bench, I listened to my lawyer, a woman who held far more faith in me than I did in myself, explain the nuances of my eighth new deal.

"John, you have to pull yourself together and do these classes."

"I can't," I replied.

She glared at me over her glasses like she wanted to shake some sense into my obstinate hide. "You're on your way to prison if you don't do what they say."

"I can't do it Rosalyn, I didn't do what they say." I launched into a diatribe that ran the gamut from my complete innocence, to misrepresentation by my dump truck lawyer, to selective prosecution and the inadequacies of the legal system ending with my own stupidity in accepting my initial plea agreement. All of which were true but mattered to no one but me.

Rosalyn waited, her slender hands folded on her jiggling knee until I had finished. She took a long, deep breath and in her sisterly way said, "John, that ship has sailed."

In that moment I experienced a realization of unrivaled clarity. I would never summon the resolve necessary to complete probation, and free myself from the revolving door of justice. I had never done fifty-two weeks of anything in my life, much less a task I was ordered to do. In my desperation I prayed for an answer and when it came to me, I surrendered, put aside all my plans and schemes, let go of my life, and gave it to God. "Get me a deal," I said.

"I thought I just did," she answered.

"Another one, a different one, anything short of prison. I'll just do the time."

She stared at me in disbelief. "You can be going home today and you want me to give up two hundred twenty-one days?"

"Not you, me. They're my days, just give them up. I do the time."

She bristled at my wise-ass reply, "Are you sure?"

"Yes, just no tail, no paper, I walk free and clear."

"Okay John, I'll do what I can."

Minutes later, I stood before the judge again; the DA had agreed to the deal but the judge was still reluctant. "He doesn't pose any danger to society, why on earth should he be locked up?" he asked both attorneys.

No one had an answer so the judge summoned my probation officer, a sweetheart of a woman, who told him,

"Your Honor, Mr. McHugh doesn't have a violence problem, he has an alcohol problem."

The judge turned and asked me why I would want to be jailed for a year when I could go home today.

I answered as honestly as I could, "Your Honor I have no home, no car, no job and no money, I have been trying to stop drinking for years now, maybe a few months in jail would do me some good."

With some hesitation he asked me to stand and rendered his sentence, a county year with a third off for good behavior, a total of two hundred and forty-four days. The gavel banged and I was sent on my way.

Rosalyn shook my hand, whispering, "I saved the days you've been locked up this time. Good luck."

"Well, three down, two hundred forty-one to go."

Arriving back at the ICP pod the same numbing dreariness washed over me. If I was lucky my next day or two would be spent here before transitioning to the main jail to serve out the remainder of my sentence. If I was unlucky, stupid, or a combination of the two, I would be remanded here until the powers that be saw fit.

This time luck was with me. The deputies scanning the incoming prisoner lists for workers paid me a visit the same day. I always worked while locked up to make the time go by faster and secure a few extra privileges, so the staff knew and liked me. The next day I was still in ICP but now as a working trustee with all the perks of the job.

Handing out sack lunches, distributing blanket rolls to the newcomers, stripping linens, and cleaning toilets comprised the bulk of my duties, but every few hours I got to dump the vomit bags of dope sick prisoners or mop the floor when they peed their beds.

The work was easy, the instructions simple, "Do as you are told."

I worked a total of about three hours during my twelve-hour shift, leaving me twenty-one hours a day to do as I pleased. I could watch TV, sleep, read, even workout. Trustees were allowed unlimited amounts of food from the deputies' dining hall, had our own library, and enjoyed the most recent DVDs, supplied by the desk officers who appreciated our efforts. There were supposed to be four trustees, but I was happy to do all the day work, so more often than not we made due with three, an arrangement that provided me the privacy of being the only inmate in a two man cell with a rarely locked door. It was as good a gig as you could hope for when you're locked up. The weeks rolled by with amiable monotony, and I vowed to grow fat as a slug, content to spend the next eight months in suspended animation, 'til my turn came to walk out the door.

About two months into my sentence, a call from Rosalyn shattered my idyllic existence.

"John, the judge wants you to go to RSVP. They have a spot open and I think you should go."

Why couldn't they just forget about me and leave me alone? RSVP stood for "Resolve to Stop the Violence Program," a dormitory in the San Bruno jail focused on anger management. I'd heard enough about these programs to know it was most likely a waste of time but Rosalyn's parting statement convinced me to at least try. "Technically they can't make you go, but if you don't go they can make you miserable."

*   *   *

The dorm door at RSVP slid open with that thundering metallic clack. I was sent to the far rear corner, top bunk, the only white face in the area. The dorm housed around sixty men most of time, nearly all with some kind of substance issue along with a domestic violence charge. The program was designed to teach us how to avoid potentially hostile situations, providing options besides punching someone if conflict seemed inevitable.

They placed me away from the other white guys to see how I would react. I said little, ruffled no feathers, and, after passing this three-day trial by fire, was moved to the opposite side of the dorm, my home for the remainder of my incarceration -- bunk 50 top, San Francisco County Jail Seven, number 2043396.

Carrying my pile of blankets and belongings across the dorm like some displaced toddler I got my first glimpse of my bunkmate. Marcel, or Cel, was at least fifteen years younger than me, an intimidating black man, six foot three, two hundred sixty-five pounds. Stretched out on his bunk, tinted glasses perched on his nose, he mumbled a halfhearted, "Whaz up?" as I climbed onto my bunk above him.

In the top bunk across from me was Alex, a Marine, almost. He had signed all the papers, shaken the recruiter's hand, bound for college, then glory or death in a trench, before his birthdays numbered twenty. A determined young man, patriotic and proud, whose entire perception of combat was gleaned from popular movies and wrestling mats after school. He had it all planned but a

145

reckless night out with some buddies and pistol turned all those dreams to shit.

Tom was one bunk over from Alex, an army nurse who somehow let one night of passion with an on-again, off-again girlfriend take him from a plush hotel to a metal bunk. At least he had a bottom rack, always a plus.

Prentiss had vowed never to return to jail, but was back in our dorm a weekv after we bid him goodbye. He'd wanted to get high one more time and was picked up in a Friday night sweep three days after hitting the street.

Ivan, or Ice as he liked to be called, was another of my compatriots. His luck had gone south during an attempted robbery of a coffee shop with a fake gun. He knew he was heading for hard times, but remained amazingly upbeat about his predicament. He would sing the Bugs Bunny song, "I got Spurs," and we would laugh and joke the hours away. I once asked him how he could be so relaxed when he was looking at five years, to which he replied, "Five years is five years, I can do it happy or I can do it miserable, I just gotta make the choice."

RSVP gave us a taste of the satisfaction that comes with achievement and improving self-esteem. Initially, I was required to take a class towards my GED. When I explained that I had graduated high school twenty-seven years earlier, with honors as a matter of fact, I was told I had to go to one class until they received documentation from my alma mater. I choose American History and marched off to class every day.

I thrived amid the chaos of the classroom. When my high school paperwork came, I was disappointed. They wouldn't let me finish the class, but my teacher, Dorian, told me I already had an "A."

In the dorm we were required to spend four hours a day doing everything from group therapy to acupuncture. The RSVP facilitators, whose job was to teach us strategies to avoid resorting to violence to settle disputes, Eric and Leo, were far from choirboys -- they had both worn orange jumpsuits just like us. They worked diligently to impress on us several key tenants of violence prevention like, keeping ourselves safe, the victim triangle, and accountability to ourselves, and others. They shared the techniques that they used to turn their lives around. I began to adopt a lot of what they offered into my daily life.

I took advantage of all the diversions offered to break up the daily monotony of the dorm. Besides the twice-weekly AA meetings, I did yoga every Wednesday night and took creative writing classes on Tuesdays. With the encouragement of an incredible teacher named Tanya Pearlman, I began to pen the first draft of this very manuscript. She was amazed at the amount of work I was able to pump out, but it was easy then, I had four or five hours to kill seven days a week.

Word of my burgeoning literary prowess spread through the dorm and, before long, even the deputies wanted to read what I had written. I could never be sure if they liked my writing, as many professed, or if they were monitoring me to thwart a rebellion or escape. It didn't matter. I was growing in ways I never would have thought possible a few short months before. Maybe there was some hope for me after all.

Anyone who has done time knows that jail is a microcosm of life outside. A small, structured terrarium where, hopefully, the inmates will somehow reform themselves and adjust to life outside by being away from it. It's time-out for adults who refuse to play well with others.

The one positive that jail, and in particular RSVP, does provide is a time for contemplation. Even amid the endless noise and complete lack of privacy, I found myself alone. I still received priceless letters from family and friends, heard of the birth of my youngest nephew, and the death of my cousin and friend from a heart anomaly -- but they were out there and I was in here. This feeling of solitude and separation began to build my self-reliance, which eventually turned into a true faith in God.

I have always believed in a higher power, something greater than myself. Who else drove me home when my blood alcohol was three times the legal limit? Or kept me alive on the freezing, rainy nights? But despite my belief, I wasn't ready to let go, to admit to myself, at my deepest core, that the sum of my bad choices had brought me to my sorry state of affairs. Which is why, even after I was released, I wasn't done drinking.

One night, after Marcel had been moved to San Quentin and I now occupied his prestigious bottom bunk, the rain lashed at the windows, and I lay relishing my warm bed instead of being waste deep in freezing water or hiding in some muddy tunnel. I had taped a small calendar to the underside of the bunk above to mark off the days until my release. I counted the days as I lay there.

In one month, three weeks, two days and roughly eleven hours, I would walk into Traveler's Liquor on 7th Street and get myself a well-deserved drink. I rolled tight in the blankets and savored the thought. I could actually taste the booze on my tongue.

The days ticked by. I worked out with Alex and a big dumb guy named Mike, I wrote like a man possessed, and did my best to prepare for what was to come, actually toying with the idea of giving up drinking. I had been given the tools, now I just had to use them.

My exit, or TX date, was set for June tenth. I had saved almost three hundred dollars from commissary money sent to me by my family over the eight months, and I was told I would have some real help with getting housing and a job if I asked for it.

The night before I was supposed to leave Leo and Eric called me to a quiet table to say goodbye and to tell me that my book would not be allowed to go with me.

"Why not? I wrote it, and I want to finish it," I declared, summoning all the techniques they had taught me to keep from exploding.

"They are afraid of what you might say," Eric said.

"I let them all read it."

"They're just paranoid they won't let an inmate leave with all that information written down," Leo added.

"Can I mail it to someone?"

"They will probably confiscate it," Eric remarked.

"Give it to me," said Leo. "I'll read it, and if it's okay, then when all the fuss dies down, I'll get it to you somehow."

Though not an ideal solution, it was better than the alternative. "Okay," I said, handing over the two hundred handwritten pages tied at the corner with a piece of broken shoelace, my greatest achievement since the birth of my son. "Thanks," I added, shaking each of their hands.

The following morning I was up before the sun, surprised to see a few other men awake well before roll call to bid me goodbye and split up my remaining commissary items. I hugged them all, gathered my few belongings, and made my way to the metal bench near the door where the deputies would round us up to go to court.

"McHugh," called the desk deputy. I rose to be shackled into the line for the bus.

"Goin' home today?" he asked.

"Yep," I answered with a smile.

"Don't ever want to see you here again," he said twisting the cuff just a little tighter for emphasis.

"You won't," I replied. So far, I've kept my word.

I was whisked through the discharge process and on the street before nine. I thought for a moment about heading to a shelter, a sober house, anyplace where I might have a chance to remain clearheaded and put my life together. Instead I went straight to Traveler's Liquors to fulfill my dream from two months before. I was free and that was a reason for celebration, Climbing aboard the Five bus, flush with cash, an appointment for GA, and of course two Steele 211 forties, I headed for the beach or the Pits, I really didn't care which. I was really free, no probation, no fines, no classes, I was finally free to drink without care.

*   *   *

I departed the bus at the Pits, one beer gone and the other open by the time I reached my stop. I ran into Pete Cummins, bound for Cindy's Liquor to buy his morning wakeup.

"Johnny Jets!" his gravelly voice cried. "They finally let you go! Welcome back!"

Pete, like many others I knew, had passed through the ICP pod while I was a trustee, so I made sure to get him some extra food, blankets and a book to read. Favors like these are not soon forgotten. He threw a dirty arm around me and pushed me down the hill to Cindy's.

"Come on, man, I'm buyin'!"

When Pete emerged from the store with a half-gallon of Jack Daniels and two big beers for chasers, the day really began. We headed back up to the Pits, and one by one the old crew emerged from the bushes, all happy to see me free, as if my release had reaffirmed all of our ability to persevere.

I was exactly where I wanted to be. I spent the day drinking with my buddies, and gathering a few blankets and other necessities I would need. I kept my cash well hidden, bringing out only a few singles at a time. I was the hero, so there was no need for me to be doing all the buying.

Tanya was a no show, everyone I talked to said they hadn't seen her in weeks. I used the time alone to build up my meager reserves of blankets and camping gear, confident that sooner or later I would hear from her.

The next few weeks were surprisingly productive by homeless standards. Eight months without a drink had given me enough clarity to at least try and move on. I kept my appointments for GA, and because I was just out of jail the whole process was streamlined -- I received a check and food stamps within a week. I spent one hundred and twenty dollars on a new cell phone, a huge investment in something I would likely lose by the week's end. The phone allowed me to contact my family on a regular basis, the first time I'd had steady contact with them in years. This first attempt at reclaiming my life proved indispensable in the coming weeks, as I soon found out that life had a few more curveballs for me.

I had left jail in great physical shape -- I ate well and worked out every day. I had even been given a physical prior to my release, which showed no need to be concerned about my health. But about a month later I began to feel poorly, sluggish. I blamed it on the heat, the crazy hours spent recycling. I tried to eat better and drank only wine or beer, but every day I felt weaker, and I knew something more was wrong.

One morning, after dragging a shopping cart filled with two hundred pounds of glass and other recycling some 30 blocks to Kezar, I waited near the gate for the 10am opening bell. My friend, Maureen, came up with her dog, Twitch, and offered me a pull on her beer. I gladly accepted.

"You look awful, John, you better get to the doctor."

"I know, I think I have the flu, as soon as I turn in I'll get to the clinic."

"Go lay down, I'll turn in your stuff," she offered.

I trusted Maureen. I had spent a night or two these past few weeks sleeping in her Dodge van along the panhandle with her and Twitch. I tried to hand her the beer back and she told me to finish it. I grabbed a blanket and headed to the soft green lawn warmed by the sun. I barely got the cloth on the ground before collapsing on top of it. The world spun and I was out in seconds. A tap on my foot after what seemed like hours roused me. Maureen helped me sit up and handed me my cash. I handed her a ten for helping me out. Her concern evident, she spoke to me more like my mother than my drinking buddy, "Johnny you have to get to the doctor," she commanded.

"I will. Let's go to Frank's and get a beer, then I'll go to the Haight Street Clinic, its right across the street."

"I know where it is, just make sure you get there. Stay out of the Pits today."

I nodded in agreement and she pulled me to my feet. We arrived at Frank's, and I waited outside holding Twitch's leash while Maureen bought the beer. I sucked mine down immediately and began to feel a little better, but I remained true to my word and went into the clinic under Maureen's watchful eye.

The doctor asked me what was wrong.

"I think it's the flu. I feel like I can't even stand up," I answered.

He placed the stethoscope to my chest and listened intently. I could see what he heard was not good as his expression grew more intense as he focused on the sounds emanating from my chest.

"Everything alright?" I asked.

"Not sure," he replied. "Let me get another opinion on this."

Soon a second doctor was listening to my chest and then they walked out of earshot to consult with each other. Retuning, they began to question me about my medical history.

"Ever have any kind of heart trouble?" the second doctor asked, straining to make this query sound routine.

"I had a heart murmur as a kid, I was seen once a year while I was growing up to check on it. When I turned eighteen or so they said it was nothing to worry about."

"You said you felt like you were going to pass out -- has that ever happened before?"

"No, not really," I replied.

"What about family? Any history of cardiac problems?" he continued.

"My dad had a heart attack and a bypass at sixty-six, and I have a cousin who just passed this year with ventricular fibrillation."

"Your cousin, what happened to him?" he asked intently.

"Kind of strange," I began. "He was a doctor on a morning bike ride with a few other doctors, they thought he just took a fall, when they went back to check on him he was dead. What does all this have to do with me?" I asked.

"Your heart beat is all over the place. We're sending you to San Francisco General. I would call for an

154

ambulance but you can probably get there faster by bus. Promise me you will go there right away."

"Sure," I answered.

They even went as far as to give me a few tokens for the bus.

"No fucking around, John, this is important."

I hadn't heard many doctors curse before, so I took the tokens and the advice, and boarded the first bus to the hospital.

This had to be a case of the doctors overreacting? I wasn't feeling well but certainly didn't think it was life threatening. I switched buses and headed south to San Francisco General, stopping at a corner store for a forty and a half-pint of vodka. The emergency room was sure to be crowded and I was not going to wait without a good buzz.

The nursing staff triaged me, and of course, I had to wait. Hours passed and the pleasant buzz I had walked in with began to fade. I stood and approached the counter. "I have been here three hours and no one has said a word to me. I am leaving."

No one seemed to care except a single nurse who took one look at me and knew this was a bad idea. "Come in here," she said, leading me into a glass-walled cubicle. "What's wrong with you?"

"The doctors at Haight Street think it's my heart, but I just have the flu, If I don't feel better tomorrow I'll come back."

"Tell me the truth," she quietly asked. "You're leaving because you need a drink?"

"Yeah, that too," I said.

"Go and get your drink. Keep it off hospital property, then come right back and I'll make sure you're seen right away. Deal?"

I had come this far and waited this long, so her proposal sounded like a good option.

"Okay, deal."

I went and loaded up but came right back as promised. In a minute or two I was on a bed in the back.

After my initial examination I was told I would not be going anywhere, that my heart was extremely weak, and I would be admitted to the hospital for a few days. Truth be told I was so sick the idea of a few days resting in bed with good food and medicine seemed like a Godsend. I was all too happy to comply with anything the doctors suggested.

The hospital staff ran tests and determined that I had some serious heart issues, including cardiomyopathy, atrial fibrillation and maybe mitral valve prolapse -- all big words that meant little to me . Again I thought they were overreacting and asked when I would be able to leave. A hospital social worker came to my bedside and I told my sad tale. No home, no money, no alternatives.

"What if I could get you into Walden House at least until you felt better?"

Walden House was one of the better known recovery programs in the Haight, but it usually involved waiting a few weeks to get in. If I was bumped to the front of the line that might work for a while.

"I would go," I answered, recalling my success at Seton Hall prior to jail.

"Let me see what I can do. I'll let you know tomorrow."

The following morning she returned, "They have a bed for you, we can get you in today."

I still thought it was a lot of fuss about nothing, but Walden seemed as good a place as any to heal up. Using a cab voucher from the hospital, I arrived at around three that afternoon, and by five the next day, I was gone.

Walden had a unique way of initiating newcomers. By treating us like children, they hoped to instill in us a sense of humility. I was paired with another resident, far younger than me, with maybe a month's sobriety. At one point I walked across a rug in a large room, and was told I had broken a rule -- newcomers had to walk around the rug, not across it.

"You have got to be shittin' me," I replied.

He then told me, that as penance for walking on the rug and cursing at him, I would have to sit in a chair by the front door until I was cleared.

"Wait here one minute," I instructed him, and since I was older, he complied. I went down the hall, gathered my things, and walked past him out the front door.

"You can't just leave," he hollered after me.

"Certainly can, just did," I hollered back, wondering if the kid would get the chair for letting me, his first charge, slip off into the night.

After a quick stop at Cadillac Liquors, I headed back to the Pits. I felt OK and soon all would be right with the world, but the next few days consisted of a slow spiral back into the misery I'd felt a week before. At San Francisco General they had told me to go to the nearest

157

emergency room if I began to feel this sick again. After three days I could barely walk up the hill to St Mary's Hospital, next to the Pits, to collapse in their emergency room doorway.

This time they admitted me to the cardiac intensive care unit. I was feisty and combative, still refusing to believe that all these health professionals were just trying to help me. One night I tried to leave and they put me in an enclosed bed, zipped from the outside so I couldn't escape. Driven by my declining physical state and my fleeting hold on sanity, all I could think of was getting away. While using the bathroom, I found a pen, slipped it into the pocket of my gown, and returned to my crib for the night. It wasn't easy in the dark but after a little coaxing I worked the zipper open with the tip of the pen, got dressed and slipped past the nurses' station. I bedded down across the street out of view. A few hours' later, flashlights were shining down on me.

"Yeah, that's him," said a barely recognizable voice.

Two policemen crouched down next to me. One of them said, "You have to go back to the hospital. If you don't come voluntarily we will 5150 you as a danger to yourself -- it's up to you."

At that point, I had no clue why I had left, and no notion of where I was going, but I did know that resisting was futile. Back in my hospital bed, I remained unconscious for two days. When I woke my doctor informed me that my heart was ready to shut down, and at his insistence the police tracked my cellphone to my hiding place in the park. He said that my "ejection fraction," the ratio of how much blood my heart pumps out compared to how much it takes in, was below ten percent and that under normal circumstances, he thought I should be dead.

I was a beaten man, released from jail on top of the world on June 10th, and given a death sentence on August 2nd.

I lay quietly in the bed praying a little, sleeping a lot. The tests ran on and on every day, my arms black and blue from my wrists to my shoulders from the constant poking of needles. They tried different medicines and little by little I began to feel better. After almost three weeks in the hospital, with no medical insurance to pay for any of it, I was released. My first stop -- Cindy's Liquor.

I don't know why I wanted a drink -- or even if I really did want one -- I just wanted to get away, to feel better. In the past, no matter how grim things got, a few pops always improved the situation. I clung to the notion that this remedy would work one more time, if only for a little while. I would worry about tomorrow when and if it came, and at that moment, tomorrow looked pretty dicey.

I can say, honestly, that I didn't want to die, but I began to feel that maybe it would be for the best. My family could stop worrying about me, the police and hospitals would have one less burden to bear; like Kelly at the bus stop, I'd be gone, and the world go on, I had taken a perfectly good life and destroyed it, and now the Piper would be paid. Even the booze had stopped working. I was resigned to ride out this last month or two, then slip quietly into the night.

I hung on quite valiantly from mid-August to October. I rested a lot, slowed my drinking to a maintenance level, and plodded through each day gathering cans. I would climb into a dumpster not knowing if I would have the strength to climb back out, marveling at the twisted irony of dropping dead in a trash heap, but acknowledging that it might be the cheapest way to get buried.

My birthday is November 1st, and my Mom asked what she could send me. At first I wanted nothing, but then I asked for a hundred dollars to keep the phone bill paid so we could continue to speak to each other. She sent the money and more without hesitation. I went downtown on Halloween afternoon to collect the cash with Big Pat and his new girlfriend, Gigi. We stopped first at the Metro PCS store where I paid the phone bill for two months, hopeful I might live long enough to pay another. Then we hit a corner store to start my birthday party. We drank and ate well, making our way back to Pat's camp near 25th and Irving. The next morning I could barely move. We climbed the small hill from the Duck Pond in relative silence, until Pat grabbed me by my shoulders and shook me like a rag doll.

"Come on, Johnny! We just need a beer then we can go to North Beach and hang out at the wharf," he shouted and shook me again, attempting to revive me.

"Are you OK?" Gigi asked. "You don't look so good."

Hearing this from a woman whose previous boyfriend had dropped dead in his sleep behind the hedges of a Bank of America just a few months before did little to bolster my waning spirit.

"He's fine," continued Pat. "Come on, Johnny, don't listen to those doctors! Hell, Lance Armstrong didn't, and he beat cancer because of it."

I failed to see to see the logic in his analogy but clearly saw the motivation for his badgering. I had money and money meant more beer. Unable to walk two hundred yards from Lincoln Avenue to Irving Street, I sat down on a convenient front stoop. "Listen, I can't go on, I'm going to call an ambulance."

"Ah, come on, Johnny, all you need is a beer!" countered Pat.

I gave him a ten to shut him up, pulled the lifesaving cell phone from my pocket, and dialed 911. Pat and Gigi stayed with me. An ambulance appeared and the paramedics leapt from the doors.

"Someone here having a heart attack?" a medic quizzed our threesome.

"I might be," I answered back.

"Why do you say that?" his partner asked.

"I have cardiomyopathy and atrial fib," I answered. "And I'm feeling mighty low right now."

"Let's see what we've got," she said, pulling her stethoscope from her pack.

She listened intently with that same serious, "this is not good face," I had seen so many times before. "We have got to get him to the hospital," she told her partner. "I can't even hear a rhythm."

They pulled the gurney from the rear of the truck. I plopped down on top of it and waited for them to tighten the straps. They gave me oxygen which felt cool and wonderful on my parched tongue. The IVs began before we left the curb. I felt exceptionally well taken care of, so I looked over the facemask, past the open rear doors, and waved goodbye to Pat, Gigi, and my life as I had known it.

The ride to the hospital was perhaps ten minutes long. This time I would be residing at UCSF Hospital on Parnassus. I had never been a patient there before but I had wandered its halls and underground parking lots to gather recycling. I was soon through the emergency room and back in cardiac intensive care.

*   *   *

They let me rest during the first two days while trying out different medicines to regulate my heart rate and get my heart function up. I said little to anyone, and then moved to a regular room where I met a pair of men who would change my life -- though for the life of me, I can't remember their names.

The first was the doctor taking the residents on their rounds. A little nerdy, a little athletic, tall, slightly curly brown hair, reading glasses barely clinging to the end of his nose, he read my history from a clipboard as all the doctors to be scribbled notes on clipboards of their own. After a few cursory questions to me, and a couple of medical opinions from them, the group left, and I dropped my head to the pillow.

A few minutes later, the doctor returned to my bedside alone and stared down at me. "Look if you want to kill yourself I don't really care -- there is a great, big bridge you could jump off right across town, but stop wasting my time. That bed you're in is for people who don't want to die."

He was right but that didn't mean I had to like it. "You know what? You're so full of shit it's running out your ears. Just because you went to school for a few years, you think you can tell everyone how to live their lives. I didn't ask to be sick. I think you are pissin' on me just to pump up your own ego! If I'm so sick, send a priest in so I can get the Last Rites. Now get the fuck out of here!"

He whirled around in a fit, the door slamming loudly as he left. A nurse came in to check on me and asked if I was all right. I told her I was fine.

Half an hour later a timid knock sounded on my door. "Come in," I said and in walked a Filipino priest. His compassionate gaze bore down on me as his chubby olive neck strained against a starched white collar.

"Why don't we talk a minute?" he began.

"Sure," was all I could muster.

The conversation was decidedly one sided, as I unloaded the mountains of guilt and remorse forged rock solid over the previous ten years. So many opportunities wasted and bridges burned, there was no way I could ever forgive myself for wasting the precious life I had been given. All the alienation, the self-sought isolation was done for one reason only, I could not stop drinking and now I had given up, I had been doing my best to hide from the people who loved me and wanted me to stop.

When you are drunk or high nobody else can stand to be near you, unless they are too. When you are not you can't stand to be near yourself. All the broken promises and missed chances, assaulting you in rare sober moments leave taking another drink, hit or fix to be your only option. The padre sat silently engulfed in my tale, it was as if he was listening on some level above the linear account I offered.

"It is never too late John," he said without judgment.

"What do I do?" I asked.

"Rely on God, have faith," he replied.

Having heard this same advice at least a hundred times before I shrugged, "What's the use?"

It seemed pointless, empty, far too non-specific to be of any use, but I didn't want to be mean to this caring man so I shook his hand and accepted his blessing and forgiveness.

After the priest left a very brave resident appeared in my doorway. "Got a minute?" he asked.

"You tell me," I answered. "The clock seems to be winding down."

"Yeah, it's not looking too good. Can I pry a little?" he continued.

"Sure, I need to make at least one friend in a white coat."

"Why do you want to drink all the time? You know you are killing yourself, surely it can't still be enjoyable."

"It stopped being fun a long time ago, but when I leave here today, tomorrow, whenever, I have nowhere to go. I'll be back in the streets, climbing in trash pails to survive. Anyone who has ever lived like that can see why a few drinks always sounds like a good idea. You see the circumstances of everyday life on the street are bad enough to stomach, but the thought of it never changing makes the whole thing feel so futile. Like you are stuck so long in a hole after a while the hole doesn't seem so bad. In fact the hole becomes home and you no longer want to leave it," I struggled to verbalize my thoughts.

"I don't get it."

"Even locked up in jail there is always a release date, something to look forward to. For me, now, there is no end to this misery, no light at the end of the tunnel, no hope left."

"There are programs, what about them?"

"I've tried many, even had eleven months sober, never quite made a year."

"Family?" he continued.

"They still love me, but they have made it clear that me drinking is never acceptable. I've stomped on their feelings long enough I would never ask for them to tolerate me another moment."

"Is there anywhere, any place you could see yourself not drinking?"

I thought hard, and decided that maybe I would try again just one more time. "There is a place called Palm Avenue Detox down in San Mateo, I was in there a couple times. I used to go there, sober up, and then go get a job, a few years back."

"Would they take you?" he asked, eyes brightening a little.

"I think so, can't see any reason they wouldn't."

"More important, would you go?"

"Yes."

"Can you call them?" he asked.

"Sure," I answered. "I'll call them right away."

"Here is the deal," he explained. "I came in here to discharge you this afternoon, but if you are willing to try and get help, I'll keep you here until they have a bed."

I could not believe what he was saying. I had no insurance, no money, and no assets at all. I had exploded at this man's boss and mentor, yet here he was likely risking his career to help me, a bum, a nobody. A lump began to build in my hardened throat. I was tired of bleeding to death while my hands clung to a shard of glass.

"You would do that, for me?" I asked, tears welling.

"Yes, make your calls."

It took three days of interminable waiting but the doctor remained true to his word. Following a call to confirm my waiting bed, I was handed thirteen different prescriptions, and a cab voucher to get to the King Street train station.

Waiting in the station, opposite the Safeway on King Street, a four-foot tall, gold and blue banner of palm trees wafting on a beach, announced Coronas were on sale, a twelve pack for only $11.99. I had never gone to a detox sober so why not buy a half case for the ride down?

And at that moment, I had a revelation.

If you have this drink, you will die -- you will never get to that detox, never stop drinking, and die.

It was true, one sip of even a lite beer would set the obsession in motion. I thought of the doctor, my family, and friends, and I stayed put, getting on the train to San Mateo as soon as it arrived.

November 2, 2005 became my new birthday. I haven't had a drink or abused any drug since.

* * *

My arrival at the San Mateo Detox marked a drastic change in my mental state, but my physical state lagged far behind. Toting more than a dozen different prescriptions, weakened by my broken heart, the mile long walk from the San Mateo station to Palm Avenue's front door nearly killed me.

Thankfully the admission process at these facilities is merciful and quick. Administrators realize that a client may not be willing or able to answer a litany of questions just in the door. Basic information is all that is asked initially, in depth interviews are left to a later date. I collapsed into my assigned bed trying to force sleep, aching for its wondrous displacement.

The effort, though earnest, proved futile. I lay awake throughout the night tortured by endless bouts of nausea and diarrhea. I spent more time in the bathroom's wooden stall than my cot. At first light of morning I went to the front desk.

"I need to go back to the hospital," I said. "I'm really sick."

A new shift had come on and the current attendant had no clue about my cardiac issues. Angry that I had interrupted his morning coffee, he seemed to think I was only looking for a way out the door.

"If you go to the hospital, you will lose your spot," he threatened.

"If I don't, I will die. Get the fuckin' ambulance," I answered.

There was no ambulance. He carted me to the San Mateo Medical Center in the center's van. While the attendant parked, I walked in, completed the intake, and departed for the waiting room. Finally my chaperone arrived and sat in the seat opposite me, still miffed about the additional attention I required.

My name blared from a loudspeaker; I took a seat in the triage area and began the initial examination. The nurse was pleasant and chatty, and all went well until she put the blood pressure cuff on my arm. "There must be something wrong with this machine," she said staring at the apparatus, tapping its side. "Let me try your other arm."

The cuff switched sides but still her expression remained the same. "I don't get this, let me do it by hand." She took my pressure again. "58 over 46 -- that can't be right. Did you walk in here?" she asked still bewildered.

"Let me try the other arm," she ordered. The result was the same and she grabbed at the phone to call for a gurney. "Are you dizzy? Lightheaded?"

"All of the above" I answered, and with that, I was back in cardiac intensive care with a new team of doctors trying to figure out what was wrong. The prognosis was bleak, I was down to 165 pounds from a solid 210 two months before. With every new medicine or modification the team tried, I grew weaker not stronger.

And then one doctor, Dr. Sangahvi, said, "John, I'm going to take you off of everything. You are taking so many different medications it is hard to tell what is helping and what might be hurting you."

Her idea agreed with everything my body was telling my brain. My system was flooded with chemicals making normal eating and sleep an impossibility.

"We will keep you off all meds for a day or two, and then we will start you back on only the essential ones, one at a time."

I concurred wholeheartedly.

The results were amazing. I began to feel better immediately. I returned to normal eating. If five meals a day is normal. My sleep patterns improved and soon they allowed me to start walking the hospital hallways, which I did continuously until the end of my stay.

I began by counting trips up and down the hallway outside my room. Soon my wandering expanded, with the hospital staff's blessing, to the entire facility. The front lobby became my home away from home, with its glass walls allowing the sunlight to warm my body and spirit. I would sit for hours reading discarded magazines and newspapers, mystified by the line of patients in wheelchairs or dragging IV bottles outside to get their smokes in. With each small triumph my confidence grew, but every step forward brought me closer to the front door.

I asked to speak to the hospital's social worker to develop an exit strategy that included a roof over my head. Melody was another ray of sunshine on the burgeoning seed of my recovery. She inquired what, if any, options were available to me upon my release.

"Well, my parents said I could go to Florida and stay with them as long as I wasn't drinking."

"John," she began. "There are two problems with that. One, the doctors need you to stay here. We finally have a handle on your heart condition and going to another hospital, never mind another state, will screw all that up. Second, you will not be able to stay sober by yourself, at your parents in Florida."

She was correct on both counts. The only reason I was still sober after ten days was I hadn't been outside a hospital.

"What can I do then?" I asked. "I've got nowhere else to go."

She told me she might be able to get me a bed at the Maple Street Shelter in Redwood City. I had heard about Maple on my previous trips to Palm Avenue. My end goal for going into detox had always been to get a bed there. It was a clean and sober shelter that allowed clients to remain for as long as six months while they worked on getting their lives together. The idea of having a bed indoors for half a year seemed like heaven to me. Shelter or not, I would make it work. I had spent eight months in jail and come out a better man for it. Six more months, working, earning money, and I would be on top of the world.

The last few days ticked by and Melody came by to see me. "John, I didn't get you into Maple yet, so what I'm going to do is give you a voucher from the county for a week in a hotel," she said.

"What happens when the week is up?"

"Call me every day at 9 am, and I promise I will get you in before the week is up. If you can't do that, you're on your own," she instructed.

"I'll call, you have my word."

That afternoon I was discharged and placed in a county van with two other men much like myself, but they were going to Maple while I was condemned to the Capri Hotel.

Like the only kid not chosen for a dodge ball game, I felt angry and betrayed when they left the van and were greeted warmly by the shelter's staff and clients, but I held solidly to the belief that my day was yet to come.

Alone in the hotel I spent a good deal of time talking with my family on the lifeline that was my phone, avoiding the isolation which often turned to hopelessness and drunken binges. My steadily improving health boosted my confidence that when I did get into Maple Street I might have a real chance to change there. I did not hesitate to share with them my newfound hope. Maple Street was different from the programs I'd been in before. They wanted you to work, and they wanted you to save your money. They knew that along with the acceptance and spirituality of the program came the reality of needing a bed and a way to eat, a concept that seems to elude many AA elders, those who had never hit bottom with the resounding thud that I had.

My brother sent me some money so, for now, eating was not an issue, but drinking was. I locked away most of the cash, taking only a few dollars each day when I left the room. I began recycling, not out of need, but out of boredom. My first day, I walked two or three miles to make less than five dollars, but I got a little exercise. It kept my mind occupied and I made it through a day, on my own, without drinking, an accomplishment I didn't think possible only two weeks before.

I developed a new mantra to focus on and guide me through each day, "Stop worrying, and just do the next right thing."

I liked it, it was practical but at the same time a little bit spiritual. For so long I had tried to control every aspect of my life, and that of a lot of other peoples', which led inevitably to failure and a litany of excuses to have a drink. Now I simply put one foot in front of the other, did my best, and left the outcome to the powers that be.

I called Melody every day as promised, and with two days left she finally had the much anticipated bed secured.

"Can you get there today?" she asked.

"Sure," I replied. "I can be there by noon."

I cleaned up the hotel room and gathered my things, avoiding the front desk on the off-chance something went wrong, and I needed my last two nights. I had hidden a shopping cart in the alleyway alongside the hotel driveway, it would be ideal for transporting my few earthly possessions to my new home.

The walk was long and hot, unusually so for a mid-November day in the Bay Area. I rested several times but my resolve never wavered as I navigated through downtown Redwood City and across the bridge above the 101 freeway to Maple Street and, hopefully, a shot at redemption.

My first impression was the standard, "Well this isn't so bad."

They gave me a "hospital bed" for a week -- not one of those high-end beds with an elevating head and foot as the name implies -- but a bed reserved for those fresh out of the hospital. Most of the good mattresses were occupied by people who had been there a while. Mine looked OK, but when I lay on it, it sagged tremendously to one side. Rather than wake up on the floor, I spun the bed to curl against the wall like a fox in its den.

My bed was located in the transitional dorm, a part of the program offering a series of private cubicles normally reserved for those who had been in the program a month or more, residents who had shown that they were serious about changing their lives, not just looking for a few meals or waiting on their next check. The intake section of the shelter, known as "Emergency," was down the hall. Like any other dorm, from summer camp to boot camp, "Emergency" consisted of two rows of bunk beds along the outside walls with a single aisle between them. It was messy, crowded, and loud, but it was the next, necessary step to securing a spot in the long-term dorm.

Two days after I arrived, I left the serenity of the transitional dorm, when a client, overcome by the combination of wanting to get drunk and having a few bucks in his pocket from a day's work, vacated his bunk in Emergency. Emergency was a lot like jail, but the door was unlocked, and there were no deputies to end disputes and quell riots. The only thing that kept them there was the fact that it was better than sleeping outdoors.

My dorm companions were not much different than my friends at Golden Gate Park's Horseshoe Pits, with the noticeable exception that, for today at least, they were sober. Sometimes that made things easier, sometimes it made things much worse. Nothing is more unpleasant than an addict or alcoholic white-knuckling through the all-encompassing desire for their favorite vice.

People constantly came and went. On any given night half the dorm might disappear, especially at the beginning of the month when many received checks. Several people stayed though, and I was fortunate enough to count myself among them. In the six months I spent at Maple, most who chose to stay became my lifelong friends, though some of their lives tragically, but not unexpectedly, were a lot shorter than mine.

Still, at first, the whole process was incredibly boring and often frustrating. My early days were spent waiting on lines in the welfare office and constantly returning to the San Mateo hospital for more checkups. If I hadn't still been sick, I believe circumstances would have driven me out the door. I was closer to my wit's end than I cared to admit.

That is when another miracle happened. I didn't know it at the time, but in hindsight, it was definitely a burning bush in the form of a bus sign.

In early December 2005, I was traveling back to the hospital by way of Sequoia Station, a transit hub in Redwood City where the county bus lines rendezvous with Cal Train. I sat on a brown, powder-coated metal bench waiting for my connection to San Mateo when a bus pulled to a stop on the opposite side of the concrete island. Above the expansive windshield was a black sign with white block lettering which read *"Cañada College"*.

I thought back to my American History class with Dorian at San Bruno Jail. I had enjoyed that class, and the opportunity to think about something other than how bad my situation was and how nice it would be to have a cocktail. In that moment I decided no matter where that bus went or what that school offered, I would be on it in the morning. I did the "next right thing," kept my promise to myself, and boarded the bus bright and early the next day for Cañada College.

The *Art of War* is an ancient Chinese military treatise, attributed to Sun Tzu, in which he states, "Opportunities multiply as they are seized." I grabbed at this first opportunity and others magically appeared.

Cañada College is a community college that sits on top of a hill overlooking Redwood City to the east and highway 280 to the west. It's a small college, but it looked colossal to me -- its physical stature insignificant when compared to the enormity of the undertaking I was attempting.

I entered the nearly deserted administration building, and followed the signs to the Registrar's Office and Financial Aid. Luckily for me the fall semester had just ended, but the staff had a few more days of work before their Christmas break. I approached the counter and a tall, young, black man who looked more like an NBA rookie than a work-study student greeted me. We shook hands as Norm asked, "What can I do for you today?"

"Well," I began. "I'm broke, homeless and staying in the Maple Street Shelter, and I want to go to school. Any suggestions?"

"Oh, come on over here, we've got to get you some financial aid."

I had never used a computer, sent an email or surfed the Web, but I sat down, and with Norm's guidance, I applied for financial aid and registered for school. "You'll get a Board of Governor's Waiver to cover your tuition," Norm said. "You should be eligible for a Pell Grant too. That will help with your expenses -- takes about a month."

Had I been left to navigate the website on my own or brushed aside and told to come back after Christmas break I would never have been in class that first day. Most probably I would have resumed drinking after or maybe while I was in Maple Street, and died in some ditch a short time later.

I doubt Norm set out to save a life that day -- he told me he was glad to help me as it broke the tedium of handling paperwork all day. I was lucky to have met him when he was bored and looking for something to do.

I started college that day a homeless bum, looking for something to help me pass the time between hospital stays. I left a full-time student. I approached the staff at Maple Street, most notably my counselor, Eric, and they said I could stay for my six months as long as I was going to school. My first Pell Grant came a month later, as Norm had promised, twenty-five hundred dollars, of which I gave two thousand to the shelter to hold for me to use when my time was up.

On January 15th, 2006, I returned to class after a twenty-five year absence. I enrolled in what I like to call my sampler plate schedule: Accelerated Spanish, American History prior to 1877, Pre-Calculus and Beginning Computer Keyboarding.

Clearly I had no idea where I was heading but I was on my way.

* * *

Over the next six months things rapidly changed for the better. I spent every day at school and every night in the safety and security of the shelter, establishing many relationships as the days ticked by. Some were long-term friendships that I hold dear today, others simply two ships passing in the night. On rare occasions the ships bumped and I was profoundly touched by someone I barely knew. I'm not sure if my increasing awareness and acuity correlated to my sobriety or to my growing connection to my higher power, but I thought less about myself and more about others and the effects my actions might have on them. One such person was another Maple Street resident, a sad soul who shared my first name.

When a client first becomes a resident of Maple Street they are given a bed in "Emergency." I was fortunate enough to get a secluded lower bunk tucked into a corner away from the main door. The only downside -- it was next to the "police bed." This bed was usually vacant so normally I had two less neighbors, but occasionally the police would find someone in the dead of night with no place to go and deposit them beside me. In the morning the occupant of the "police bed" could speak with the staff about a longer-term arrangement if they were, at least for the time being, done with sleeping on the street. Which is how I came to know John Hockett.

Around one a.m. the dorm door creaked open and in came John. Small in stature with a whiny sort of voice, he exhibited a "Rainman-esque" list of behaviors that placed him in the *really* crazy category as opposed to the partially or perhaps temporarily crazy like me. He yapped endlessly to himself, circling the bed, adjusting the pillow and blanket twenty or thirty times before turning in. Then he began getting in and out of the bed -- each trip doubling my skyrocketing blood pressure. Finally he left through the side door and sat at a table just outside the dorm to commiserate with one of the day sleepers -- residents who stayed up all night then slept all day.

The next morning, deprived of the better part of a night's sleep, I walked into the kitchen around five am to hear John happily announce, "I don't do drugs, I won't ever do any drugs."

I angrily interrupted, "Listen, motherfucker, you better start taking some drugs because I won't put up with your shit again, ever. Do you understand me?"

John looked at me not afraid, but bewildered. Spinning back to the dorm, I heard him earnestly tell his fellow nightowl, "Something's wrong with him. What got him so mad?"

Over the next few weeks, as hard as I tried not to, I got to know John. I didn't get the factual details of his life, like where he was from or did he have any family, I got to know *him*.

He spent half the night on a broken cellphone, talking to the police, reporting those who had done him wrong during the day. At first I thought this was a ruse to keep people from bothering him, but as time went by I began to think John actually believed he was in communication with law enforcement.

"Hello officer, yes, he is right here, yes, he threatened to manhandle me, and you're on your way, good," he might say, then announce to the world, solely for the benefit of the culprit, "That's it, he's coming, you'll see, you will see now, you are going to jail, my friend."

He spoke endlessly about his need to find a "good Christian home." He came to our recovery groups sometimes just to sit, sometimes to talk. He spoke of things that happened years ago as if they were going on today, because in his head they were.

John left the shelter on the first of the next month armed with the money from his disability check to begin his pursuit of a good Christian home. He returned several days later badly beaten and penniless. The director of the shelter bent the rules and allowed him to return without the normal waiting period. His eyes were black, his bottom lip swollen like a grape, his head and face viciously scratched as if he had been dragged, face down, along a sidewalk. He did not know or could not remember what had happened or who hurt him.

The police took a quick report, the animal that beat him went unpunished, and I begged God for forgiveness for my callous behavior that first night. John was more than *really* crazy, he was mentally ill. Maybe he flashed a wad of cash that led to him being robbed. Maybe he said or did something that angered someone, but he didn't know any better. Beating him was like beating a child who could not comprehend what was going on. My thoughts returned to that first night when I wanted to strangle John for interrupting my precious sleep. I understood that his maddening compulsions were not an attempt to aggravate me. Perhaps the shelter was the only place he felt safe enough to speak without the threat of someone hitting him. Another piece of my ego crumbled as I realized, at times, I had not been much better than the scum who'd beaten him.

John stayed at the shelter several times during my six months there. He would come and go, no plan, no cure, just existing, imprisoned by his own mind. I got together with a few of my more notorious friends and we put the word out that anyone who hurt John would get ten times worse in return; the police knew this and kept an eye out for him as well. We did what we could to keep him safe. At one point I tried to apologize for yelling and threatening him that first night, but he couldn't remember, so I made my amends in other ways. When I would see him wandering around town I'd get him a burger or a doughnut, whatever was close by.

Occasionally, he would remember me. About a year after we met my parents visited me for the first time in California, and outside a K-mart, John came up to say hello, dirty and disheveled, but still in one piece.

I introduced him as he told my mom that he was still searching for a good Christian home.

I asked, "How about a nice Jewish home?"

He thought for a minute, then nodded. "I guess that might work too," he decided aloud.

I gave him a five for a Little Caesars' Pizza and he took off happily for the store.

My mom, a little perplexed, asked, "Who is he?"

"Just a friend from the shelter," I replied.

Some of my friends were harder to like than little John, but they too changed not only the way I thought, but the way I believed.

In all my days of living on the street, in shelters and jail I have never met a man nor heard a story which compelled me more than John Murphy's.

Murphy was a bad ass, a tough guy, a bull of a man, average in height but built strong and solid like a fireplug. His broad shoulders, bulging forearms and calloused hands told the tale of thirty years of hard work. A lack of any type of formal education belied the intelligence hidden beneath the gleam of his shaved black head. He was the product of shootings and stabbings. Of years lost to the pen and his desire for heroin. Still he was a stand-up guy, the kind who paid back the money you loaned him even if it always took a little longer than he had promised.

Often incensed by how little life offered, which he of course deemed unacceptable, Murphy would launch into a tirade. A fit of door slamming and chair kicking accompanied a stream of profanity vile enough to shame a prison guard.

Into the dead of night he would rant, "...took twenty cops to take me down, you muther fuckers don't fuck with me! I don't play like that; I ain't never gonna play like that..."

The other occupants of the shelter dorm either cowered in fear or waited dispassionately for the storm to subside, depending mostly on how well you knew him. Usually things ended as quickly as they started, with the realization that his keys were in his jacket pocket or the recovery of a lost shoe.

In the end it took only a few speaks of powder, a gram or two of "China White" to bring him down for good. He was an easy man to hate, which many did. There was however another side to the man, a side not nearly as easily discerned.

We sat one evening outside on the smoking area bench just opposite the pay phones, cars slipped by on the freeway a short hundred yards away. The whine of their tires hypnotically rising and falling like the surf at Ocean Beach in the balmy twilight of the peninsula, amid clouds of smoke curling languidly from his lips Murphy relayed to me a series of events he'd been involved in earlier in the day which resulted in the expulsion of a young girl from the shelter.

"Johnny, you ain't gonna believe what she did..." he said, the volume of his voice dropping to conspiratorial levels.

182

My mind strained along with my ear. What could this freckle faced wisp of a woman possibly have done that would cut him to the quick?

He paused for effect, gathered himself and said, "That bitch called me a Nigger."

I stifled a laugh as I realized that this was no joke, he was completely serious. A comment he had undoubtedly heard hundreds of times before, a term that all the young gangsters called each other with glee in jail, one that I was guilty of muttering into my pillow during his nighttime tantrums had hurt him so deeply.

"How could she say that John? I ain't never done nothing to her." He asked biting his bottom lip.

He sat crestfallen, a little boy with his broad shoulders slumped, the wind sliced from his sail by the tongue of a child he could snap like a matchstick.

"I don't know Murph," I replied, "what was she thinking.

In his own way Murphy was a valiant man. Raised in a world of dope deals and the consequences that inevitably follow them he struggled, at least when I knew him, to leave the mess he called his life behind.

Ten years old was too young to be admitted to the shooting gallery at the end of the East Palo Alto Street, even the dealers and the junkies had their scruples. The ten dollar bill taken from the purse of a jaundiced mother, whose eyes glowed yellow like a banana, was just enough for a slender mocha arm to gain entrance through a busted out back window. He looked to the ground awaiting the pin prick, followed first by a wave of nausea, then at last the warm euphoric rush coursed through his veins. Still in grade school, on the rare days that he decided to go, he was hooked on a drug powerful enough in the hands of a surgeon to allow for removal of an appendix or amputation of a gangrenous limb.

It would be a great injustice to say that the deck was stacked against him. It was the deck, the table, dealer and casino as well. For the next thirty-five years through a series of arrests, incarcerations, jobs gained and lost, family members delighted at clean time then destroyed by relapses, Murphy fought to regain the control he had relinquished through that broken window decades before. In the end the drug won. Demanding, relentless, rapacious, the fix I'm sure he swore would be his last, finally was.

I saw him last two weeks prior to his death at the local 7-11 getting a coffee before beginning his day at yet another new job. He was clean inside and out, having shaved both his head and the scrubby stubble that covered his chin when we met at the Arco station a week before. The dilapidated Honda he had been sleeping in was replaced by a beige four door Buick Century not nearly new but definitely a step up.

"I still owe you ten, right?" he asked.

"Keep it," I answered shouting above the roar of a landscaper's truck exiting the store with three

Mexican laborers crammed into the cab beside the driver. We exchanged a headshake and bemused smile.

"No, no I'll get it to you," he replied.

I departed with a wave, he flashed a right back at you, putting the Buick on the roadway heading south.

I guess now like before it's just going to take a little more time.'

Two weeks later I got the word Murphy had died. I will never forget my friend, his story and the tremendous impact it had on me and my recovery.

* * *

My life began to take on a sense of normalcy as my time in the shelter accumulated. I went to school each morning, came home for group counseling in the afternoon, and attended AA meetings three evenings a week. The counseling group, though mandatory, was something I would have happily done anyway. It was run by Rich, a fellow alcoholic and ex-jock and nearly all the clients who regularly attended the group completed their six-month stay. The people I was closest to were Alberto, Dave, Milano, Edene, Giselle, and Mary Ann, and while they were all extremely special to me, Milano John, a Czechoslovakian madman I came to love like a brother, took the proverbial cake.

I first met Milano skulking about the men's room at Maple Street. He was wide awake at the crack of dawn obsessing over his daily chore of mopping the floor and cleaning the sinks, hours before anyone else at the shelter had begun their day.

"You need bathroom?" he queried in a thick eastern European accent, as if I might have some other more sinister reason for standing there barefoot in boxer shorts.

"Yep," I answered in a disoriented, sleepy timbre.

"I just clean," he added eyeing me suspiciously. With a wave of his right hand, he indicated the gleaming countertop.

"I'll keep it that way."

I slipped into the stall and plunked down on the porcelain throne staring at the black work boots and bottom third of a denim clad leg posted inches outside the door.

"Every morning I get up at five to clean and by nine bathroom is shit."

"Well a lot of people have to use it," I remarked in a vain attempt to pacify him.

"No! They are peegs!" he barked, his accent dragging out the word "pigs" making it even more vile and insulting I tended to more pressing matters as Milano's vigil continued to deprive me of even the smallest measure of privacy. He rambled on about our fellows, our peers in poverty, each observation beginning with a belittling description of the perpetrator, like, "Fat girl who drink all the milk that is for cereal, she is peeg."

"Stupid guy put sneakers in dryer make noise all night," which, for Milano, translated to half past nine at night to five in the morning.

I tidied up and headed back to bed. Without turning I could feel him inspecting the stall as I left, and I made a mental note to steer clear of this head case

Milano went out of his way to create controversy and then wallow in it. Some mornings his attitude could spoil milk. He was always battling one agency or another. His full name was Milano John but everyone instantly inverted it to John Milano. He continually parlayed this error into bills he refused to pay. He would max out credit cards and then insist that he didn't have to pay because, "Name on card is wrong, that is not my name." Milano delighted in not paying when, "Azzhole at company fucked up!"

Despite his antagonistic behavior many people liked him, and liked him a lot. Milano exuded a naiveté that could be quite charming when he wasn't cursing you out. His eccentricities may have stemmed from his upbringing in Communist Czechoslovakia. In Milano's world institutions -- government, banks, hospitals -- were all corrupt and/or incompetent and deserved to be exploited.

Regular people were good and he helped many including me, but put a regular person in a uniform or behind a desk and they became the enemy, hell bent on depriving Milano of something, anything.

Milano and I completed our six-month stays at Maple Street in June 2006. Our friendship grew steadily over our six sober months there, despite our first meeting in the bathroom. I called him "Kamush," Czech slang for "pal" or "buddy." He loved when I would listen to his latest tale, lower my head, and slowly shake it side to side, sighing a hushed, "Kamush," in a "What am I going to do with you?" tone.

"That is puurrfect," he would add, smiling from ear to ear. "Just like real Czech guy."

Milano started drinking again almost as soon as we left the shelter. As he drank the charming part of his personality evaporated -- he became the bitterness.

In typical white trash fashion, I purchased a large RV to call home and moved to a trailer park. Milano followed close behind, moving into a trailer a few doors down. At first his exploits were comical; over time they became pathetic. I tried to keep an eye on him, to minimize the damage his boozing inflicted. Driving home I would see a pile alongside the road. Stopping, I'd find Milano had fallen off his bicycle or collapsed in a drunken heap. I would haul him into my pick-up, throw the bike in the back, and deposit him in his bed.

Very early one morning I drove past his trailer to see him stumbling down the steps in hip waders, propping himself up with his prized Benelli shotgun. "Just where do you think you're going?" I asked, approaching slowly, eyes fixed on the weapon, wondering if he had thought to load the gun. Something that sounded like "Hunting," was his slurred reply. I took hold of the gun and twisted it from his grip. "Come on Kamush, back to bed." I took the gun and kept it under my mattress; Milano never asked for it back.

His decline continued with two more stays in the shelter followed by increasingly devastating relapses. Seizures set in, as Milano couldn't keep enough alcohol in his body. Even six hours spent sleeping would deprive his body of the precious juice and he'd awake with violent shakes, every cell in his body screaming for more alcohol.

I stopped in to see Milano one morning hoping to catch him sober; he was broke, trembling terribly in need of a drink. I remembered that feeling of utter despair, knowing the drinking had to end, yet needing that drink so very badly. I drove him to the liquor store and bought him a half pint of Smirnoff and a forty-ounce beer, hoping that he could "get well" before a seizure hit. It proved to be too little too late. As we drove home, Milano erupted in a violent Grand Mal episode. I threw my right arm across his chest, pinning him against the seat, while wrestling the truck to the shoulder with my free hand. His body bounced forward, his eyes rolled up showing only the whites. He emitted a low, strangling sound as all the muscles in his body fought against each other. I held tight, staring at the floor thinking that, somehow, if I wasn't watching, he wouldn't die in my arms. Finally the veins in his neck became less pronounced, the convulsions diminished, and I sped to the hospital as he drifted into unconsciousness. At the emergency room entrance I tore open his door, and he looked up at me with an expression of pure helplessness that I will never forget. An aide brought a wheel chair and we took my buddy, my Kamush, into the ER.

The aide gagged as we cut away the putrid clothes he had been wearing for weeks. He had soiled himself in every way possible. We cleaned him up and they strapped him into the bed, resting pillows against the bedrails to protect his head. I went to the triage nurse who insisted Milano had never been treated there before.

"Look up John Milano," I instructed and the computer screen lit up like Times Square on New Year's Eve.

Milano spent about a week in the hospital. At first the effects of the seizure along with the drugs he was receiving, made it impossible for him to even recognize me. I toyed with the idea of leaving him there to become someone else's problem. He left the hospital one afternoon, with or without medical clearance,I don't know. I found him passed out in bed, a half empty fifth of Royal Gate vodka open on the table.

Milano called me one day, at the height of his drinking, weeping that he had a problem he could not fix. He begged me to meet him at his trailer. I stopped by after work, elated by the possibility that my stubborn friend may have finally seen the light. Perhaps I could get him to Palm Avenue or any detox willing to take him -- I understood now there was no way he could quit cold turkey without risking a seizure or even death. At least now we had a chance at another miracle. I banged loudly on the trailer wall. Milano, sullen and ashen, appeared in the doorway and sat down on the painted metal step just below the door. He reeked of booze, and head in hands, tears carved rivulets through the dirt on his face. I approached slowly and placed my right hand on his slumping shoulders.

"What's going on Kamush?" I asked, waiting to finally hear him surrender, to hear that he was truly powerless, an affirmation that only the alcoholic can make, the true first step towards rebirth and salvation.

Between the gasping sobs he finally pronounced, "My DirectTV is not working!"

At that moment, I gave up hope. I didn't abandon him, but I knew the end was inevitable and inevitably going to be bad. Like when someone has terminal cancer and you pray for a miracle but are pretty sure one isn't coming. I said a silent goodbye to Milano, leaving him in God's hands. He drummed up some money, and moved to a cheaper trailer park where dope deals and booze ran rampant.

Before his drinking began in earnest Milano had loaned me a thousand dollars to buy the very same pick-up that took him to the emergency room that March morning. When he called looking for money I always offered to send him the entire grand, but no matter how dire his circumstances, he refused to take it. I don't know if he was afraid of the spree he might go on with a windfall of cash, or if I would wash my hands of him because I no longer "owed" him, but he never willingly accepted. During one school break, I paid his rent for a few months to balance the books, hoping that, maybe this time, things would be different. They weren't, and another year went by. Milano would call every week or two to talk or if he needed a few bucks.

On Memorial Day weekend 2009, the Santa Clara County Sheriff's Department phoned to tell me Milano had been killed the night before, struck by a lightrail train.

His body was crushed beyond recognition. They found my phone number in his wallet, the only clue as to who he was and who might know him. His blood alcohol content was high enough to kill most people, and the poor, distraught train operator who watched him plunge beneath his wheels was found completely blameless. I helped the police locate a Czech friend who called his family, since no one spoke the language, to relay the sad news. His remains were cremated and entombed in a pauper's crypt. He was gone and no one cared.

At first I couldn't grieve him. I was in the middle of finals week and needed to focus and concentrate, but found I could do neither. I would stare at a page, trying to get through it, but could remember nothing. The harder I worked, the worse it got. I was so filled with rage. My only thought was, "That son of a bitch. His dying act was to fuck my life up." My grades came and I squeaked by in every course but one.

Two weeks later, back in class, a new set of challenges faced me. Milano remained front and center in my mind. No longer angry, I started to miss him. I had grown to love him, did all I could to help him, yet I could do nothing to relieve the pain in his heart. The tears finally came and with them a small epiphany that strengthened my faith -- Milano was better off dead. My acceptance of this fact released me from the guilt and helplessness enveloping me. It was as if God looked down and said, "My child I have given you so many chances, I can't allow you to go on suffering, it is time to come home." Then he lifted Milano's spirit from its mortal coil and took him to find the peace that had eluded him in life.

He is one of many guardian angels who watch over me each day.

*　*　*

In recovery in general and more specifically in AA, people constantly point to those who get *It*. As a newcomer this is maddening. You go to a million meetings, do the twelve-step shuffle, bare your soul to others, beg for forgiveness from those you would just as soon smack in the head, and yet *It* still eludes you. Members smile broadly at those who really get *It*, as opposed to those who are beginning to get *It*, or the truly unfortunate who had *It*, then lost *It*, but they will never tell you what *It* is. No one, not even those claiming fifty-year chips at birthday meetings, knows what *It* is. The closest approximation might be Louie Armstrong's answer when asked, "What is Jazz?" He replied, "If you have to ask what Jazz is, you'll never know."

Edene got *It*. Together from Day One at Maple Street, partners in temperance, we graduated Maple six months later alongside a still sober Milano. During the second month of our stay, Edene got a job interview. a huge event at Maple Street, a bittersweet turning point on the road to recovery.

On the afternoon of Edene's interview I met her, running from her car in tears, halfway up the concrete walk to the shelter's front door.

"What's wrong?" I asked.

"This girl's just not ready," she sobbed.

I threw shelter protocol to the wind right there in the main lobby, and wrapped her in the biggest bear hug I could muster.

"It's all right," I said pulling her tighter to console her, "There's no rush, take your time."

From that day forward Edene held a special place in my heart. I never asked what went wrong at her interview, figuring that if and when she wanted to tell me, she would, but from that afternoon on we were all but inseparable for the better part of the next two years. She was part confidant, part co-conspirator, part sponsor and always one of my best friends. During that first year sober, when even the little everyday things can overwhelm you, when the structure and rules of Maple fade into the past, she became the concrete surrounding the cornerstone of my recovery.

Though she had completed her time at Maple Street she wasn't quite ready to return to her old life. I didn't have much to offer, just a pull-out couch behind the driver's seat in my RV, but we became roommates for the next year and a half. We knew basically all the same people, went to many of the same functions, shared stories about the various lunatics, fought to keep Milano from killing himself, counted the others who were not as lucky as us. Eventually, after a little coaxing, she also went back to school and earned an associate's degree in Medical Administration. I know I shouldn't take any credit for this, but I can't help thinking my example showed it was doable.

*　　*　　*

My last couple of months at the shelter passed smoothly. I made the honor roll at Cañada and began doing small carpentry jobs to make a little extra money. Next door to the shelter was a large boatyard housing Jim's Diesel Repair Service. I didn't know Jim but after watching him scrap several old, wooden boats I offered to remove any salvageable pieces, like portholes, cleats and rails. These parts, made of copper, brass and stainless steel, were highly sought after by boat enthusiasts.

"Can't pay you," Jim declared. "I've been down this road before with guys from Maple."

"I'll do it for the rest of the scrap," I offered hoping the leftovers would justify my efforts.

"Let me get this straight," Jim asked. "You'll pull the good stuff off for me and I'll let you have the rest?"

"Yeah, wire, pipes, manifolds, any scrap. I'll make a pile and take it to the yard every week or two."

"Okay," Jim said, and we shook on the deal.

I worked for Jim a day or two each week, keeping my precious metal piled in a corner between two packing skids. After two weeks, I loaded the scrap into a friend's truck and hauled it to the scrapyard. I made almost $800, gave my driver $50 for gas and an hour's work, and returned to tell Jim the good news.

I was sure Jim would be as surprised as I was at the value of the scrap. Broken down by the hour, I made around $40 an hour. Jim might be delighted with my good fortune but he might also decide it was worth $800 to eliminate me and return the scrap himself. I thought about keeping my news to myself but worried about what would happen if he eventually found out. After a little consideration I decided the "next right thing" would be to share the windfall.

I crossed to Jim's office and banged on the door. "Here Jim, this is for you," I said handing him $200 in crumpled bills.

"What's this for?" he asked, eyeing the stack of bills.

"The scrap was worth a lot more than I thought, so I figured we could split the extra cash."

"That wasn't the deal," he stated, incredulous.

"Forget the deal, this is more than fair."

With some of the money I saved, I bought an Old Dodge RV for $500, one of the crowning achievements of my stay at Maple. The truck ran well enough, but the RV was literally falling to pieces. I came up with a plan to create a work truck from the wreckage, and backed the rig up to the boatyard fence opposite Jim's office.

On Friday night I set to work, covering the truck's camper section with a large blue tarp. I ran an extension cord through the chainlink fence to Jim's office. The Skillsaw and Sawzall made short work of the cabinets and structure, and by Monday the tarp was flat on the deck of the truck. All that remained of the 26-foot camper was the cab and rolling chassis. It took me another week to fabricate a wooden truckbed.

Now mobile, I had a dozen ways to bring in a little more cash, starting with gathering pallets to sell. The truck held about 50 pallets in six, neat stacks. At $2 each, I earned $100 every time I found enough to fill the truck. I ran errands for Jim, helped people move, hauled cardboard and scrap to the recyclers, hustling any way I could to make a buck.

About this time Edene got a job at a local costume shoppe, the place was insane, aisles of elaborate disguises, racks of practical jokes and gag gifts, row upon row of weaves and wigs, customers just a little crazier than her co-workers. She fit right in. At one point her boss, Jack, needed some shelves built and I became the official carpenter/handyman of House of Humor. My wooden truckbed now served as a mobile workbench, and my collection of tools grew at a staggering rate.

Still marveling at how quickly things seemed to be turning around, I got another offer from one of my cohorts in the afternoon HALO group.

Dave Bernie grew up on the Peninsula and knew every half-assed criminal in a twenty-mile radius. He was also a talented electrician who shared my obsession with alcohol, a trait which made him, at least for the time being, unemployable.

Dave thought otherwise. Always one to think big and sweat the details later, he approached me with the idea of starting a construction company, inspired, he believed, by none other than the Almighty himself, perhaps as a reward for the two of us remaining sober for all of four months. I listened intently then tried to curb his enthusiasm with a brief summary of the facts as I saw them.

"Dave, we're two bums, living in a shelter, one of which owns a thirty-year old, rolling tool chest, complete with bad muffler and bald tires, the other with a 1989 Ford Taurus with maybe a quarter million miles on it, and a trunk you open with a screwdriver. No one is going to hire us."

"Johnny, you worry too much," he replied. "I know lots of people. We'll get work, in fact, I have a job we could start right now if you want."

"What job?" I asked, his confident reply piquing my interest.

"A big one."

"OK, I'll bite. What do you have in mind?"

"My sponsor, Doug -- I've known him for years -- wants to put a deck and extension on his house. I told him I knew a guy, you, who could build the thing. I'll do the electric. He knows where we live, John. What do you say? Think you could do it?"

"Yeah, I think so. What does he have in mind?" My reply was quick, confident, typical of a man who knew exactly what he was doing, but I hadn't worked on a real project in a decade. I thought of a thousand ways this undertaking could turn into a disaster.

"He wants to extend his bedroom, add a bath, and put on a deck that opens to the kitchen and bedroom."

"Sounds like a lot. We would need plans, permits, inspections -- the whole nine yards."

"Yeah, I told him not to worry, you'd figure all that stuff out."

So tentatively, I stuck a toe back into the contracting business. We met with Doug on a foggy Saturday afternoon in April. Doug called the fog God's air conditioning, which made me smile and I liked him immediately. He wasn't what I expected. Dave referred to him as "my sponsor," instead of "my friend," so I expected a much older man, but in fact, he was a little younger than Dave, and nearly thirty years sober.

We went over the basic layout of his dream home. He reached for a pen and paper to write everything down. "I got a bad case of CRS," he explained, flicking open a pair of readers, and perching them on the end of his nose.

"What's that?" I asked with genuine concern.

"Can't Remember Shit," he replied with a laugh.

I thought long and hard before accepting Doug's offer. Without question I once had the skills and ability to see the project through, but five years of living in the woods had sapped my last ounce of confidence. Still, like returning to school, the opportunity offered another rung up the ladder of respectability. I accepted the job with a self-directed pledge to finish what I started, no matter what.

Our initial progress was slowed by the permitting process and my inexperience dealing with the ins and outs of the building department, but the dedicated staff in South San Francisco took a liking to me and directed me along the path. Within two weeks I produced a full set of plans. We secured all the necessary documentation and Doug wrote the check to the town for nearly two grand. Now I was in deep. No longer a notion, the project had evolved into a full-scale responsibility. I arrived early the following Saturday with a tape measure, shovel and string line and by Sunday evening the footing trench was finished. The project was officially underway.

Over the next few months my life blossomed, evolving in leaps and bounds. My education, now in its third semester, migrated to the City College of San Francisco on the advice of Arturo Hernandez, my then counselor at Cañada. He pointed out, quite correctly, that at forty-six years years old I shouldn't waste precious time deciding on a major. I chose Architecture and CCSF had the best nearby program. There I was introduced to delineation, rendering, and design, learning the creation phase of projects I already had the hands on skills to complete.

Just before starting at CCSF, I got a fortuitous call from Leo Green, my RSVP counselor at San Bruno Jail.

"How have things been treating you these past few months?" Leo asked.

"Not too bad, Leo. I had some health issues but I'm staying in a sober shelter, working a little and going to school. In September I'm starting at CCSF," I answered, omitting the three months of drunken debauchery prior to my heart problems.

"That's great. I've got some good news for you too, I have your book in the trunk of my car."

His words took a second or two to sink in. Aside from my one creative writing class I hadn't thought much about my manuscript what with school and all. The stack of pages that had been so important to me a year before had slipped into the "I'll get to it someday" corner of my mind.

"I can meet you any Saturday," Leo continued. "Can you get to the city at all?"

"Sure Leo that's not a problem. How about we meet up by the Cal train station on King Street?" I asked to avoid driving the hulking wooden flatbed into downtown.

"Eleven o'clock will work for me, how about you?"

"Perfect I'll be there," I replied.

That weekend I made my way north to the King Street station directly across from the Safeway whose discounted Coronas nearly derailed my recovery and ended my life. Leo was waiting as promised. We spoke only briefly as he had double-parked. "You look great John. I read a little of your stuff -- it's really good," Leo said with a smile and handshake.

"Thanks Leo, thanks a lot. I still have a lot of work to do but just getting this back means the world to me. You and Eric have helped me more than you will ever know."

"Just keep doing whatever it is you're doing and you'll be fine."

"I know I will Leo." I nodded, staring at the scruffy pile of handwritten pages clutched tightly between my hands.

"Well I've got to get moving before they arrest us both for blocking traffic," Leo kidded me. "Take care, John, and keep up the good work."

"I will Leo." My voice cracked a little, as I choked up for the first time with some measure of pride. Leo and Eric's small gesture of returning my manuscript enabled me to gauge my own progress, by reviewing my past through my own eyes, an indispensable discipline in the years to come. It's human nature to block out the memories of misery and pain, but doing so allows the door to a relapse to open a crack. Now I could delve into the pages of my past and see how far I'd come. I liked the man I was becoming.

Having weathered my jail time, begun rebuilding my life at Maple Street, moving forward with my education, I started to realize that what I thought of myself, my own self-worth, was far more important than what others thought of me.

Prior to my second divorce and my move to California I lived my life to make others happy, assuming that if those around me were happy, by extension, I would be too. I tried to find fulfillment as a husband and a father, but I wasn't very good in either role. Now I defined myself by my decisions and my accomplishments, things that I wanted to achieve for myself, not things that I "had to do" or did because I had no other options, not what my wife or parents wanted me to do.

One fact that became abundantly clear to me as I finished my time at Maple Street was that I performed better as a solo act. I would never have returned to school had I been in any kind of relationship. My attention would have been focused on my significant other rather than the work I needed to finish for class.

The hardest part of continuing my education was not getting distracted. The higher education race is won through endurance and perseverance, two qualities I sorely lacked until my second go-round at college. When I returned to school I had nothing, so it was easy to focus on the assignments, but as I worked and saved a little money, caught a wink or two from different women, got a car, then an RV, it was harder and harder not to pursue making more money and a little companionship.

Up to this point I accomplished a lot by maintaining a forced solitude that left me with little else to do but study. I still traveled to San Francisco to see Tanya, now with a new man, Andrea, or the boys from the Pits, but I always returned home to the shelter and later on, my RV. These oases gave me a buffer zone, compartmentalizing my life and allowing me to leave the past in the past. No one questioned me about leaving if I said I had schoolwork to do and no one wanted to be the person who convinced me to stay and ended my recovery.

*　*　*

During my last few months at Cañada, I decided to take another trip and booked a flight to New York to see my entire family while my Mom and Dad were there visiting from Florida. I hadn't been back in at least five years and had never been there sober in my adult life. My flight there was the first time I stayed on the wagon while traveling. This did not happen by accident. To ensure that I arrived sober to see my family, Doug took me to the airport, I got on an earlier flight which was already boarding, flew non-stop to LaGuardia, where Tom, my brother-in-law, picked me up and took me straight out to Long Island, allowing little time or opportunity to screw up.

They treated me with kid gloves, and I can't blame anyone for being overly concerned with my potential to self-destruct. I stayed close to my sister's house, wasn't allowed to borrow a car without my parents in tow, and was delighted when Tom dropped me at the airport to return to California and my summer session classes.

A delay in my flight left me with three hours sitting in a place in which I loved to drink, a pocketful of cash, and no one meeting me on the other end. I'm very comfortable with flying, but I always had a few pops before getting on a plane, and the thought of doing that right then was very, very appealing.

One thought prevented me from imbibing. I had to start classes the next day. I knew in my heart that if I had a drink my return to school was over. In the past I would have concocted some plan to allow myself to drink, but maintain a slim chance to stay in school. I would have emailed my teachers explaining that a family emergency

202

had forced me to remain in New York a few more days, but I would be in class bright and early Monday morning. This would leave me until the weekend to drink, then get my shit together and show up.

Then I realized that I truly believed if I took that one drink I would never stop until I died. Clearly I still had one more run in me, but I definitely didn't have the capacity for another recovery. I had played my last ace in the hole. My head was full of AA, future goals, and growing accomplishments. The depression and self-loathing that would follow a drink would cripple me forever. The booze was no longer attractive, I didn't need it, didn't want it, and the obsession lifted.

*   *   *

Summer classes were limited so I took two General Ed courses -- English Comp and Public Speaking -- to fulfill a requirement for transferring to a university, my end game. In English Comp we were required to write a half dozen papers, and instead of slapping together an introduction, body and conclusion, I actually took the time to craft an interesting piece. The instructor, Susan Gangel, liked my writing so much she suggested I join her creative writing class the following semester.

While drinking I was Hemingway, Kerouac, and Hunter S. Thompson rolled into one. In Susan's writing class, I developed the skills to prove I had at least a sliver of their talent to go along with our shared debauchery. My writing continued to improve and I was published in the Cañada campus magazine.

The Public Speaking class required us to stand at the front of the room and give three 10-minute speeches during the semester. The first of these was designed to introduce ourselves, and share with the audience some personal information along with the usual name, major, and career goals often used as ice breakers in new classes. I decided to tell the story of my addiction, or at least the Reader's Digest version, for the first time publically.

Public speaking is a nail biting undertaking, especially when baring your soul. "Less than a year ago I was lying in a hospital bed," I began. "Listening to a bunch of doctors recite all the reasons I should be, and shortly would be, dead. I couldn't have cared less. All I could think about was getting past them, out the door, and up the street for a drink."

The expressions on my audience's faces went from courteously disinterested to mesmerized as I relayed my journey from jail to living on the streets. The last few minutes of the presentation required a question and answer session so I wrapped up my speech and braced for my interrogation.

The room fell silent as people gathered themselves to politely ask the questions they obviously wanted to ask. Finally one woman, Maria, a little older and more self-assured than the rest spoke up, "John, congratulations, on how far you've come. Can you tell me what made that one day different, the day you finally stopped?"

"In my case, I think it was more than just a day. I didn't have a revelation, a burning bush moment where my eyes were opened and everything changed, it was more the cumulative effect of all the consequences, coupled with the therapy and rehabilitation I had been receiving which allowed me to finally decide enough is enough."

The floodgates opened. I answered questions from nearly everyone in the room, including our professor, until our class time ran out. Everyone seemed to have a brother, sister, cousin, or friend faced with the same sort of substance abuse issues. People clamored for solutions, something they could do or say to turn a loved one's life around.

I returned to my seat to applause much louder than the congratulatory golf clap normally given to departing speakers.

I knew then that I had something to say, something that people wanted to hear. I spoke with several people after class and received a hearty handshake from the professor. Just outside the classroom, Theresa waited to speak with me privately.

"John, can I talk with you a minute?" she started.

205

"Sure, what's up?"

As we descended the stairway to the courtyard she began to open up. "Well, it's like, I try not to drink too much when I go out, but I always do. My friends have two or three drinks but then they stop. I say I'm going to stop too, but I never do."

I listened as she shared her shame, the list of behaviors I knew so well -- hiding booze, drinking and driving, swearing to only have one drink and loosing count after ten. When she finished I could have bombarded her with statistics on the harmful effects of drinking, or explained that some people, like myself, and quite possibly her, have a genetic predisposition to alcoholism, but she didn't need a lecture. She needed help and reassurance that she was not evil or damaged.

"Listen, I think if you are wondering if you have a problem, you just may have one and you should check it out."

"How can I do that?" she asked. "Without everyone hating me?"

"No one hates you, in fact, I have a friend who just might like to talk to you."

I wrote Edene's number on the cover of her notebook and gave her a little hug.

"This is a friend of mine, just a little older than you, who stopped drinking same time as me. I'll let her know you're going to call. Just give me until tonight to let her know."

Her eyes plead with me not to abandon her, so I lifted her notebook again and put my number right below Edene's. "If you need someone to talk to before then, call me anytime." A smile crept across her lips.

"I'm pretty hungry," I continued. "Want to get something to eat?"

"Yes, I'm starved," she answered, her smile widening.

We spent an hour in the cafeteria, and then I walked her to her car. Theresa seemed content to have the start of a plan. I phoned Edene and apologized for giving out her number without asking first, explaining that I didn't want my intentions to be misconstrued. As I suspected it was not an issue and Theresa called her the following morning. They became friends, and Edene eventually became Theresa's sponsor. Occasionally I would see them at meetings together and during class I would sometimes get a thank you smile from Theresa.

* * *

Dave Bernie and I became even better friends as the work on Doug's house neared completion. After leaving Maple Street, he was lucky enough to receive a year of housing assistance from the County of San Mateo. With the county footing the bill for two-thirds of his rent, he secured a nice little apartment in the quiet community of Belmont, just north of Cañada, and immediately began acquiring the trappings of luxury he felt he deserved -- a nice, four-wheel drive Ford Ranger pickup, diamond jewelry to win back his estranged wife, all the accoutrements that shout, "I am not a bum, I am something special!"

Dave even moved his son, Joey, down from Stockton to share in his good fortune, bringing him to Doug's to teach him to be an electrician, but this proved more of a challenge than he bargained for and Joey was soon working with me.

Joey was a really good kid, conscientious and hard-working, but he lacked the mindset necessary for working in construction. Although a good part of the job is simple manual labor, in order to move past lugging lumber for a living, you must develop an increasingly diverse skillset. Joey wanted to please his Dad, but he could have cared less about learning a trade.

When the job at Doug's ended, his next-door neighbor, Doris Vincent, asked me to replace her house's collapsing stoop and re-side the residence. Joey tagged along as my helper, but eventually I ran out of work for him, and he started living half-time in Stockton, and half at Dave's.

Dave had a history of back problems. After back surgery at Stanford Hospital, he seemed different, a little off, which Doug and I attributed to his recent operation. He slept a lot and became harder and harder to get a hold of. Finally, after not hearing from Dave for three days, I stopped by his place on my way to school.

His truck was parked in the carport beneath the apartment so I climbed to the front door and banged loudly. No one answered. I pounded on the door again. Joey should have been there but there was no sign of him either. At last, I twisted the doorknob, it turned easily in my grip. I cautiously opened the door, shouting for him and Joey as I peered over the threshold.

Dave lay dead on the floor beside an open fifth of E&J Brandy, shirtless, his skin a ghastly blue grey, with one sock on, and the other clutched in his petrified left hand. He was so skinny, like a cross between a dead bird and an Auschwitz victim.

I stared at the open bottle perched on the table two feet above my dead friend. No one would blame me for taking a swig, not after what I had just walked in on, the relentless rationalization continued. The desire for displacement nearly overcame me, as I fought the urge to hoist the brandy. I stepped back out the door and pulled it shut. Grabbing my phone I called Doug.

"Doug, it's me. I just found Dave at his place and it's not good."

"He's drinking again, isn't he?"

"No, not anymore. He's dead."

"Are you sure?" Doug asked.

"I'm sure. He's lying on the floor half-dressed, there's a bottle on the table, and it looks like he's been there a while."

There was no response, just intense silence followed by a low sigh of resignation.

"You're the first person I called," I said to fill the void. "Guess I have to call the cops now, huh?"

"Yeah, they're going to want to check out the scene," he answered. "Do you have time for that?"

"I'll make the time. I can't just leave him here."

"Are you okay?" Doug asked. "That's a hell of a thing to find."

"Yeah, I'll be alright," I replied, keeping my urge to grab the bottle to myself.

"John, call me again if you need anything, anything at all."

"I will, but I can handle this," I said to bolster my own confidence. "I'll call you back. Bye."

"Bye John, love you." At first I thought his expression of affection odd -- Doug had never bid me goodbye like that -- but then I realized that Dave's death, our partner in crime and recovery, brought us closer than we had ever been; now we always say goodbye like that.

The police arrived half an hour after I called 911. I told the operator there was no rush, Dave wasn't going anywhere. The first officer on the scene was kind of a dick, pulling me to the front of his cruiser to pat me down and question me. I was no newcomer to these tactics. Not sure if I should even reply, I chose my words carefully.

"Why would you come over here to check on him?" he asked.

"I needed him to finish a job we were working on, he wasn't answering his phone."

"When did you last see him?" he continued.

"Four days ago at the job in South San Francisco."

"You haven't been here at all since then, didn't even drive by, maybe last night, night before?"

"No." I didn't like the tone of his questions, so I compressed all my answers into single words.

210

"Are you guys friends, I mean away from work?"

"Yes."

"So you know him pretty well? Ever have a fight, an argument, I mean over work or anything?"

"No."

As the cop tried to reword his questions to entice me to divulge more a second car, a dark blue, unmarked Crown Vic, pulled to the curb. Another officer, obviously one with some rank, left the vehicle and walked to my side.

"Captain," the inquisitive officer said with a nod. "This is John McHugh. He found the body. Seems they knew each other from work."

"Thanks, I'll take it from here." The captain politely asked, "Can you spare a few minutes?"

"Sure," I replied, sticking with single syllables.

"Can you tell me how you found him?" he asked.

"I am in recovery, Dave was too. We are, well we were, working on a home extension for his sponsor in South City. He hadn't shown up for work in a few days, wasn't answering his phone so I decided to check on him this morning. I was afraid he was drinking again, which he was, but I never expected this."

"You guys were in AA?" he asked.

"Yes. I knocked for a few minutes, then I tried the door because I saw his truck parked down below. He was laying right there when the door opened."

"Did you go inside?"

"No, I could see he was dead so I closed the door and called 911," I answered, relieved that I didn't touched the brandy.

"I know a few people in the program," the captain added. "You need anything?"

211

"No, I was on my way to school. Do you guys need me all day?"

"No. We have your phone number?"

"Yes, and my address. I'm at Trailer Village in Redwood City."

"You head out to school, if we need anything we'll contact you."

I drove home instead. Doug called to tell me that Joey had gone back to Stockton the night before, following a big fight with his Dad, after he had started drinking again. Edene was as surprised as I was; Milano, who was still on the mortal side of the great divide, swore that he knew Dave would start drinking again. Something about Dave not paying him back twenty dollars he had borrowed, and Karma being a bitch.

"Did you ever ask him for the money or remind him about it?" I made the mistake of asking.

"No, that is not my job, and now he is dead."

The mystical implication was clear. You did not want to find yourself on Milano's bad side.

Two days later I helped Doug, Dave's ex-wife, Karen, and Joey clean out Dave's apartment. We threw out the bed, and sent the couch to Maple Street since they'd paid for it in the first place. Doug and I snatched a few mementos, then boxed up what was left. There wasn't much. We packed Karen and Joey's cars with anything of value.

"What are you going to do with the truck?" I asked Karen.

"I can't afford it," said Karen. "The payment is $350 a month."

"I can take it back to the dealer if you want," I offered.

"Sure, John, thank you for all the help."

The dealer, Rich, was shocked to hear about Dave, saddened at losing a friend and customer. Recovering quickly, he stared at the truck. "You want it?" he asked me.

"Sure, it's beautiful," I replied. "What would it take?"

"Just send me proof of insurance and make the payment every month," he said. "That way I don't have to redo all the paperwork and you won't need a down payment."

"The truck stays in a dead guy's name?"

"Sure, I don't care who makes the payment and we can leave it that way until the registration comes due."

"I'm good with that. When I have to deal with DMV, you'll help me out?"

"Sure, if you make every payment on time, I can redo the loan, get a better rate. I liked Dave, but his credit was horrible."

"What a shock!" I replied with a handshake, then climbed into the cab of my shiny, silver, four-wheel drive, extended cab Ranger.

The days following Dave's passing brought back many of the same emotions I felt seeing Kelly Harper trussed up in a body bag at Ocean Beach the year before -- the pointlessness of it all, and the lingering notion that I could well be next. This time, however, they didn't feel as ominous and unavoidable. Dave was dead because Dave forgot he was an alcoholic and an addict. His drug of choice was always more, more of whatever he could get his hands on. We're all going to die, but when you get a second, third, even a tenth chance, continuing to tempt fate is moronic. With each relapse we face ever-increasing odds that this one will be our last.

Joey called one day, fighting back tears, to tell me about the fight he had with his father the night he died.

They hadn't come to blows, but Joey lost his temper and stormed out and returned to the safety of Stockton. "I should have stayed there with him," Joe lamented. "Maybe then he wouldn't be dead."

"No Joey, you did the right thing. As soon as your dad chose to drink again the end results were out of your hands," I explained. "Please don't beat yourself up over this, you were a good son and he loved you very much, it's just sometimes the obsession is too big to overcome."

We shot the breeze for a little while longer. Joey told me about his new job working at the local Safeway. "They made me a senior customer service representative," he shared proudly.

I couldn't have been happier for him, and although I remained upbeat on the phone, the thoughtlessness of Dave's actions enraged me. I despised him for reestablishing contact with Joey only to break his heart one last time. I vowed never to do the same to my family, especially my son.

Driving home from Doris's house a few days later, I received another call. I pulled off the 101 and answered. "John," the unknown voice began. "I was hoping I could ask you a question about Dave's death?'

"I'll be happy to help if I can, but just who am I speaking with, please?"

"It's Mrs. Bernie, Dave's Mom."

We had met briefly at Dave's funeral, but I could not begin to guess to what mystery I held the key. "I spoke with Karen and Joey, and they said you would be the one to ask, being you found him and all. Forgive me for being blunt, but was Dave's death a suicide?"

I thought for a minute, then answered, "Not a chance Mrs. Bernie. Dave was far too fond of himself to try anything like that."

"Thank you, I just didn't know who else to ask."

I felt the need to expound. "At the apartment it looked like he was getting ready to go somewhere." I left out the grisly details and added something else that crossed my mind, which I hoped might comfort her more, "Maybe over to see you and Mr. Bernie."

Dave hadn't said anything about seeing his parents that day, but he visited them fairly often. Even if I was wrong, who could it hurt? I wanted to offer her all the comfort I could in that moment since, most likely, I would never speak with this woman again.

                          *   *   *

Armed with my bright, shiny, new-to-me four-wheel
drive I returned to San Francisco the following Saturday,
and parked near the Pits to show it to anyone I could
round up. As I climbed the hill I noticed a slumped figure
on a fallen log just off the trail. The figure's voice was
unmistakable. "Johnny Jets, come on over and sit a spell!"
Pete called out. Between his legs sat a pair of Olde English
40's and a fifth of Jack.
    "Hey Pete, what's up?" I asked cheerfully, though Pete
clearly wasn't in the best shape.
    "Guess you heard about Bob," Pete said.
    "No Pete, what happened?" I'd spent two months in
jail with Bob Pardini. In the woods we'd nearly come to
blows several times, but while in jail and sober, we'd
become close friends.
    "He died," Pete stated matter-of-factly. "You want any
of this?" he added, pointing to the booze between his feet.
    "No Pete I'm fine. What happened to Bob?"
    "Good, good for you, Johnny." Pete continued, "Bob
died of liver cancer about a week ago. They found it two
months ago, told him if he stopped drinking he might live
another two years. He laughed at them, said he had been
drinkin' for forty years, and he wasn't about to stop now."
    "Sounds like Bob," I said as Pete lined up his booze
soaked thoughts.
    "Yeah they said it mertaster ... matasti ... metastasized
-- God that's hard to say -- anyway he was dead in a few
weeks."
    "That sucks," I said. "How you feeling with all this?"
    "Alright I guess, pretty tired now though."

I didn't mention the truck or any of the good luck I'd been experiencing in light of Bob's demise and Pete's disoriented grieving. Instead I offered Pete a way out. "Hey, why don't you come with me for a few days? Clear your head. I don't care about the drinking, you can just get some rest. We'll talk later."

"Nah, Johnny. That stuff might work for you, but I'm too far gone," Pete answered. "Just need to lay down for a few hours."

I lifted the sagging Pete by the arm, stuffed his precious bottles in the bag they came from, and helped him waddle off into the bushes. He pulled a pile of ragged blankets from the brush and plopped down in the center of them.

"Good night, John," he said though it was well before 11 am.

"Good night Pete," I replied, pushing his bag of bottles beneath the blankets so no one would see it and swipe it from him.

Pete died two weeks later after overdosing twice in four hours. He had been speed balling heroin and crank, probably for days, and was rushed to Saint Mary's ER, revived by a Nar-con injection, and discharged an hour later. He returned to the Pits, picked up right where he left off, and overdosed again. Not quite as dramatic as leaping from the Golden Gate Bridge into the freezing waters of San Francisco Bay, but suicidal nonetheless.

In the recovery game the deaths of three close friends in quick succession is a double edged sword. The left half of my brain, the rational, analytical part makes the obvious connection between picking up a drink or a drug and the probably fatal outcome.

The emotional brain, however, craves the release that only a good buzz can provide.

"What's the use?" becomes a mantra as all one's choices seem utterly pointless.

Although I was keenly aware of this phenomenon I was categorically unprepared to deal with it. A feeling is not like a thought or idea, easily dismissed with the shake of one's head, it is a lingering cloud which grows thicker and more consuming the harder you try to combat it.

I called Doug, the closest thing I had to a sponsor. As I relayed my dismay at the steady departure of my friends and the feeling that I was some sort of unwitting Grim Reaper, Doug listened patiently. "John," he began. "You have to realize, we are the miracles."

"Huh?" I replied.

"The chances are pretty slim for anyone to really recover, most people think that it's a given if you sincerely want to stop you can, but the true alcoholic or addict will continue using until, as the Big Book says 'They stand at the gates of insanity or death.'"

"Really? It's that bad?"

"In AA, they claim a 70 percent success rate, but from what I've seen over the years, I would guess it's more like 10 percent."

"I guess they count the dead ones as no longer drinking," I laughed.

"Probably. An old timer once told me he would ask guys what their shoe size was before he agreed to sponsor them, that way he was sure to get something out of it."

"So you and I are the miracles, huh?"

"Yep."

"Well somebody certainly lowered the bar."

Talking with Doug seemed to take away the power of the urges, revealing the lunacy that taking a drink embodied.

The longest I had ever gone without a drink prior to this was eleven months -- I had wanted to make a full year but fell short by a few days. Now, with nearly two sober years in the books, I was definitely sailing in uncharted waters. I had come to trust in my higher power to guide me and would pray each night for direction. I never asked for specific things only that I would be shown the path, and granted the fortitude to follow it. The solutions were there for me to find if I just did the next right thing.

One such solution emerged from a potential disaster as summer drew to a close.

I had been working smaller jobs often given to me by independent contractors, mostly punch list work to enable them to collect final payments. I was quite good at both finishing the job and, more importantly, satisfying the customer. One of these contractors, a handyman named Tony, pushed my patience to the limit. He had seen me in the Home Depot parking lot and asked if I could finish a handrail on a freestanding staircase for him. The job, though a little tricky, was well within my skill level and I assumed Tony's as well.

At first I thought Tony simply didn't have enough time to tie up the loose ends, but when I arrived at the first job he was waiting. I thought he wanted to check out my work but as the handrail progressed it became obvious he had no idea how to begin the job much less complete it. I finished the job and the happy customer handed Tony a stack of hundreds. I thought payment wouldn't be an issue. I was wrong again.

"John, I have some other bills to pay but don't worry I've got a ton of work for you. How 'bout I'll give you half today and I'll catch up next time?" he asked.

While the request annoyed me, it wasn't the first time I needed work badly enough to wait for full payment.

"Alright," I answered. "But only this once, I'm the broke college student here, remember?"

Tony did not remember; in fact he did his best to forget. At the end of each job I finished, he would give me just enough money to keep me hanging around to do the next job. He started instructing me to pick up material at building supply stores, saying he had an account or had already paid for the supplies. More often than not there were no payment arrangements and the follow-up phone call would be ten minutes of him begging me to pay, which I never did.

Finally at one lumber yard the cashier said loudly, "Are you kidding me? We won't let that guy charge a pound of nails." He went on, telling me about a half dozen bounced checks, and at least as many promises to pay off his delinquent account.

At that time Tony owed me $1300. My options were limited, but two things were clear -- I wasn't working for him again, and one way or another, I would get paid. I called constantly, set up three meetings that Tony failed to show up for, and finally decided a message needed to be sent.

Through the miracle of the Internet I traced Tony's fictitious business address on Market Street to a nice apartment in Diamond Heights. All the debris I had removed from his jobs sat stacked high in my pickup, a sight which tortured me no end every time I climbed behind the wheel. Returning all his trash to him seemed only fair, so I drove to the city at midnight and piled it on the hood and roof of his truck.

No longer hidden by fake addresses and phone numbers, Tony coughed up the balance of the money he owed me. "John, I'm really sorry for the mix up," he said. "I have one job I need you to estimate. It's a big painting job for me, probably $1500, but I need you to do some woodwork first."

I took the phone number with no intention of calling. A week went by and I refused to return any of Tony's two dozen calls. The siding job at Doris's house was winding down and in an effort to keep Alberto and I working, I pulled the number from my wallet and dialed the number.

"Hello, this is Bill."

"Hi Bill, my name is John McHugh. I'm a carpenter. Tony asked me to give you a call about some woodwork you need done."

The line remained silent for so long I thought we'd lost the connection.

"What the hell is wrong with that guy? Do you know what I do?" Bill barked. Before I could say a word, he answered his own question, "I I run a construction company! He was supposed to call me two weeks ago, now he conned you into coming over to look at the job?"

I could see this was going nowhere fast. "Look I don't really know this guy, but I could have used the work. I'm sorry to have wasted your time. Have a good day."

"Hang on," Bill said. "Why don't you come by anyway? He wants the painting job, but there's no way he's getting that."

"Okay," I said and took the address.

I took Alberto and we finished renovating Bill's front porch in a few days. While waiting for him to arrive home after work I caught up on some calculus homework in the cab of my truck. A knock on the window broke my mathematically induced trance.

"You're doing Calculus?" Bill asked.

"Yeah just Calc 1. I finished pre-calc last semester so now I'm working with derivatives," I answered, surprised at Bill's ability to instantaneously decipher the mathematical hodge-podge on the page.

"I didn't know you were in school," Bill stated. "What are you studying?"

"I'm at City College doing architectural technology. I hope to transfer to a university at the end of the year."

"That's great, John," he continued. "You know I'm the Chief Operating Engineer with my company."

That was all it took to start a friendship with someone I really came to admire. Most of my friends were of the blue-collar variety, Bill had that side to him too but he was polished and professional as well. I liked that about him and wanted the same for myself.

I never told Bill about my life in the woods or that I had camped alongside Lake Merced across the street from his house for a few weeks until the police ran us back to Golden Gate Park. The first time he became aware of it was probably reading these very words. He knew I didn't drink and never asked why, I told most people it was due to my heart condition which ended any further discussion.

Occasionally someone might say, "Oh you can't drink?"

To which I would respond, "No, I can drink just fine, it's the stopping part that gives me trouble."

Bill trusted me and I was never going to give him any reason not to. Having someone I could ask questions about school and pattern my career choices after proved invaluable.

*   *   *

September 2008 Cal Poly Begins

At San Francisco City College, II had been working towards a transfer Associates' degree in Architecture. I applied to several universities with a licensed Architecture program, among them Cal Poly Pomona, which accepted me with a catch -- I had been wait listed for acceptance into the Architecture program; technically I was number 42 in 40 seat program. Advisors from both CCSF and Cal Poly assured me that at least two people would choose another program, so I planned my move to Southern California.

I traded the Ford Ranger for a Toyota Tundra and sold the large RV in favor of a slide-in camper for the Tundra, outfitting the rig with a pair of deep-cycle golf cart batteries, a power inverter and satellite TV. And then I said my good-byes.

Aside from Andrea, I was glad to leave the Bay Area nonsense behind me. All my friends had far more than the usual amount of baggage, and though I stood by them through some tough times, I was glad to move away. I was not yet strong enough to set the boundaries necessary to deal with the chaos created by others. Although it sounds selfish, the only way for me to move forward was to focus solely on myself. The crux of my recovery had become my education.

For the next six years Cal Poly Pomona became my home. In late July, I drove to my 3-day orientation, sleeping in the bed of the Tundra at rest stops along the I-5 and in the Glendora Home Depot's parking lot, with a one night stay aboard the Queen Mary in Long Beach Harbor to celebrate my transition into a university. I drove

223

at night and slept mostly during the day as the police would come by and bang on the truck's side at night to inform me that resting was allowed but sleeping was not. It was all a matter of how comfortable you got. It was OK if you remained in the cab with the seat reclined to take a nap, but if you were fast asleep, especially at night, with an air mattress and pillow in the back of the truck, that was too close to camping and you were sent on your way. The officers were very friendly and constantly let me know that they were "just doing their job," so I would move along immediately.

By the time the semester began, I had installed the slide-in camper on the truck and paid for two weeks at the East Shore RV Park, a fantastic facility perched above picturesque Puddingstone Lake in the Frank G. Bonelli Regional Park. While the campground was the perfect spot to stay, it was a nuisance to pull up stakes every morning to drive the three miles to school, and return at night to reestablish camp. I knew a twenty-four hour computer lab was about to open in the school library, and as soon as it was finished I decided to remain on campus full-time.

As opening day neared, I stayed on campus for two days to see how the Campus Police would react, then went over the hill to Home Depot for a night, and returned to school for two more days. I carefully selected a different parking spot each time, and left the area completely over the weekend. After a month of this routine I became complacent. I stayed a full week without moving the camper, and slept late on Saturday morning. As punishment for my sloth, a loud knock woke me around 10:00 am.

Though I dreaded this first meeting with the Campus Police, I knew it was inevitable, and did my best to take things in stride. To my surprise, so did the officers.

"What exactly is going on here?" posed by the policeman without stripes on his sleeve.

I decided to go on the offensive. "Hi Officer. My name is John McHugh. I'm a student here. I'm 48 years old and I was staying at the RV Park up the hill, but I have two labs which keep me here 'til 10:00pm Tuesday and Thursday, so it seemed silly to leave that late. And with the computer lab open all night I can get work done any time I want."

The officer asked for my license and student ID. He called both in over his radio. "Looks like you're okay," he stated. "But we have had people trying to live here in cars before and it usually doesn't work out. Anyone else staying here with you?"

"No, it's just me. I have to take medicine for a heart condition, and sometimes it makes it hard to drive. That's why I stayed the first night, and then no one seemed to mind," I said, playing the medical card to better my odds of being allowed to stay on campus.

Finally the senior officer who had remained silent stepped forward and said, "Listen, we don't really know how this is going to go. We will speak to our commander and see. Until then you're fine to stay, but mind your manners. No mess, no one else here, and no drinking. We will see how it goes from there. Got it?"

"For sure," I replied. "Thank you for the chance."

"We can't promise anything," he reiterated.

After a handshake they were gone and for the next six years they never bothered me again. In fact I got to know some of Campus Police quite well. I was constantly upgrading the truck, and even bought a larger step van during my junior year. They would come by to see what new project I was working on, admiring my ingenuity, and asking how I was doing academically.

One of the officers remarked, "I can't wait 'til my kids are in school. There is going to be a town out here." For just this reason I kept quiet about my arrangement. The last thing I needed was a whole bunch of newcomers spoiling my good thing. In my senior year, a reporter from the Poly Post left a note on my windshield requesting an interview, but I politely declined. I didn't want the officers to get in any trouble, or start an avalanche of copycat campers.

Occasionally the Campus Police would ask me to keep an eye out for a suspicious vehicle, or tell me when events like the Dog Show or Indian Powwow were going on at the campus. They were really good guys who helped me more than they will ever know. At the time, nine months in the dorms cost over $10,000 and there was no way I could afford that.

Living accommodations aside, my progress towards a degree was steady, but not without a few curves. The first curve involved my choice of major. No one had opted out of the Architecture program, which left me with two choices. One, take a bunch of general electives and hope to be admitted the following year, or two, change my major to Civil Engineering.

The decision was a no brainer. I had been debating the pros and cons of Engineering versus Architecture since returning to school anyway. Engineering offered a more pragmatic and practical approach to design, while architecture offered greater freedom for creativity. Even though it meant taking a plethora of math courses, including two more levels of calculus, and linear algebra, I declared Civil Engineering, with a Geospatial option, as my major. I grinned from ear to ear as I left the Registrar's office, just like I did when I became a student at Cañada. I envisioned how far I'd come, from piecing together makeshift campsites in Golden Gate Park, to developing designs for actual bridges and buildings.

My first year classes were pretty easy -- chemistry, some calculus based physics, lots of labs, and a few introductory Civil classes, including Elementary Surveying. During my first surveying class, my group of four included Jeanette, Pachisa, and Jeff. Pressed for time at the end of our lab, I told Jeff to go hold the rod on the point we were shooting. After setting up the instrument I looked around. Jeff was nowhere to be seen.

"Jeanette, do you have any idea where Jeff went?" I asked.

"No, John. Should I call him on the walkie-talkie?"

"Sure. We are running out of time, and I'd hate to fail on our second project."

Jeanette called Jeff several times; finally his voice squawked over the walkie-talkie. "What do you want?" he asked.

"Where are you, man?" I asked. "We have to get this done."

"I'm over near the steps in the shade. It's too hot out there in the sun."

I screamed into the handheld radio, "What? Get your ass over to the damn spot and hold the rod up straight!"

"OK, OK, stop screaming," said Jeff.

As I muttered a few F-bombs under my breath, I turned to see Jeanette backing away, afraid to speak following my tirade, and I realized that I would have to temper my actions and language. It was easy to revert to my construction site foreman ways, hollering orders at a bunch of regular guys making good wages, but my classmates were kids just out of high school. Being around them on a daily basis made it easy to forget they were so much younger than I was and I was forced to acknowledge that this was their time, their world, and I was just an incongruous visitor to it.

Jeff, thankfully, was pretty thick skinned, and had the advantage of being two hundred yards away. Again the walkie-talkie crackled. "Did you get the shot? I'm sweating over here."

"10-4," I answered.

"What?" asked a bewildered Jeff.

"Yes, come on back."

Almost any other guy would have been annoyed at me calling them out during the exercise, but Jeff could have cared less. I had a newfound respect for him and his devil-may care-attitude. At the same point in the Civil Engineering program, we ended up having many classes together and began to seek each other out as partners for projects and tests. Often we'd score the same on tests, with the only difference being that I studied a lot, while Jeff barely cracked a book. One day I asked him, "How do you get this stuff so quickly without studying?"

"John, I've been in school since I was eighteen months old. Taking one test seems the same as another."

We remain friends to this day.

* * *

Throughout that first year at school I remained in constant contact with all my San Francisco friends. Sammy and Milano called nearly every day. I'd shoot the breeze with them and, depending on what their feelings on recovery were at that point, I'd relay what worked for me. They loved to talk about getting sober and working towards the things they wanted, but with no real commitment from them, it was essentially a waste of their time, though I now believe that these conversations were critical in remaining sober myself.

Every alcoholic, like me, thinks there is some way that he or she will be able to achieve all the trappings of a normal life and still be able to drink. At this time I was two years sober and, once in a while, I would still get the notion that picking up a drink might be fun. It could be a beautiful, sunny day when my school load was light, just after midterms or finals, or it could be after hearing of yet another death in the City by the Bay and feeling, as the saying goes, that I "really needed a drink." However, something had changed deep inside -- I had passed the mythical point of actually believing my own bullshit. All I had to do was think about the mountain of guilt that would result from abandoning my sobriety, play the tape all the way through, and feel the despair and self-hatred that always followed a "harmless drink."

There is another AA-ism, "When you let the gorilla out to dance, he decides when the dance is over." Sobriety is dull; it is agonizingly boring to sit for hour after hour in AA meetings, rehashing the same reasons for drinking, and the strategies for stopping, over and over in my head. Letting the "gorilla" out was an adventure, one that

229

usually ended badly, but an adventure nonetheless. School filled the void created by my abstinence, kept the gorilla in its cage by filling my time with classes, studying, and new relationships. My choice was simple -- I could have a drink or I could get my degree.

During Spring Break of my freshman year I arranged to meet up with Doug and spend a few days in Las Vegas. After picking him up at the airport we headed for Sin City, the acid test for sobriety. Milano had just died and spending a few days with Doug seemed like the right thing to do. We gambled late into the nights. I played nickel slots and a little blackjack, while Doug fed twenties into the slot machines like he had printed them up in the hotel room closet. We ate good, laughed a lot, and didn't drink a drop. It wasn't until after I had dropped Doug off at LAX that I realized I had a ton of fun without any booze, I hadn't even missed it. Another tentacle of my obsession no longer wrapped around my throat.

* * *

Summer 2009

The school year ended well with my GPA a solid 3.3. I made my way back to San Francisco and my summer job delivering Bounce Houses. I hunted down a few of the old crew during my first weekend back. After dropping off a birthday jumpy at a party near the duck pond in Golden Gate Park, a familiar hoot echoed through the trees. As I turned the corner I saw Big Pat standing between Black Joe and Charlie. "You guys look like an Oreo cookie," I shouted from twenty yards away.

At that distance they didn't recognize me. The trio immediately went into mean mug mode. "Who's doing all that talkin'?" Black Joe shot back.

"Not even gone a year, and you guys forget me already," I answered.

As I approached, Charlie's scowl began to soften as he recognized me. "Johnny! Johnny Jets! Where you been? They lock you up again?" he spit out in his staccato delivery.

"The one and only," I replied. "And no I haven't been back to jail."

Pat rushed me and hoisted me from the ground in a huge bear hug. Joe followed suit but did not attempt to lift me. Charlie settled for a hearty handshake, and we retired to the log to commiserate.

"Johnny you look great, still not drinkin'?" Joe asked right off.

"Yeah, Joe. Coming up on two years now," I replied.

"Where you staying? Still down in Redwood City?" he continued.

"No I moved down to LA. Pomona actually, right on the edge of LA County."

"What do you want to live there for?" Charlie chimed in.

"I go to school there, C, at Cal Poly. I am going to be a civil engineer."

Following his initial war whoops Big Pat had remained uncharacteristically quiet. Finally he opened his mouth, but instead of words he just blubbered, as his eyes filled with tears. "I missed you, man. Things ain't the same around here anymore."

I gave Charlie some money and he took off to the store for the customary bottle and my now habitual Diet Pepsi and peanut M&M's.

Pat recounted his versions of Bob's and Pete's deaths. Though slightly different from the stories I'd already heard, the main points remained consistent, leading me to believe what I had been told was true.

"Johnny you got to come by and see my place," Joe said with no small amount of pride. Through years of persistence, and now Section 8 housing, he had finally secured a one-room apartment downtown, but took the bus to the log each day. Some nights he still slept in the bushes behind the log too drunk to wander home.

"Where are you hiding these days?" I asked Pat.

"Behind Arco. They know me pretty well, and I get some money every morning by helping people pump gas."

Whether Pat actually assisted people or they just gave him a few bucks didn't matter. He had found a home and as the guys at Arco surely found out he wasn't going anywhere.

"Listen, I'm setting up the Bounce Houses again this year. If you can behave yourself, I can use you as a helper."

Pat smiled broadly, "Really Johnny, I would like that."

"Sure, but if you start smoking rock there is no way I can keep you around."

"I hear you, but I haven't done any in almost a year," Pat stated, more to convince himself, because I wasn't buying it.

Charlie returned with the refreshments and asked to borrow my phone. I handed it over; he called his family in North Carolina. I never hesitated to share my phone with Charlie. Once I loaned it to him while I was quite inebriated, we got separated and I forgot about the whole exchange. Two weeks later, having given the phone up for lost, Charlie drew it magically from his pack.

"I kept calling my Mom till it ran dead, Johnny, hope that's cool," Charlie said.

"No problem," I answered. "The minutes are free and I'm just happy to have it back."

That's how things were in the woods. New faces appeared, but it took years to build trust. Even people I'd known for years could only be trusted as far as I could spit, but my core group of friends from the Pits and the beach had banded together to make the going a little more bearable for each other. Whether it was sharing a wakeup to quell the DT's, or offering a blanket and a place to lie down on a cold, foggy night, these small acts of kindness formed the attachments I could not let go of when I became sober. It was brutal to watch the slow demise of one after another of my friends, but I couldn't just leave. I had given my word to help, both to their faces and through my involvement in AA.

Big Pat worked with me, disappearing as soon as I handed him some cash, and I started bring Alberto along as an insurance policy. Sammy begged me for work, so I let him help me out a few times until one morning, shortly after picking him up, he announced, "I can't work today. I was up all night smoking crack and you know how hard that is. Think you can pay me now?"

I wanted to smack him and scream, "Pay you for what? Are you fucking kidding me?" Instead I gave him a twenty to which he replied, "Ten dollars an hour? I can't work for that."

That was the last time he accompanied me.

Although well-versed in addictive behaviors, and extremely tolerant when it came to my buddies helping me, I could not understand why they couldn't reign in their outrageous behavior for a day or two. I let them drink beer all day, but it wasn't enough. Not enough of a buzz, not enough of a rush. Their addictions had grown to include a litany of drugs -- Pete died of an overdose of speed, Pat could not put the crack pipe down, Sammy was addicted to everything from alcohol to Afrin, and that's just the A's. Gone were the days of simply drinking until passing out, then getting up the next day and doing it again. Pat was even given phenobarbital to curb his seizures, but threw it away, because, as he said, "I can't even catch a buzz on that stuff."

Later, I came to realize I had set the whole cycle in motion. My friends needed work, which I gave them, but I didn't want to be a bitch and insist that they not drink. I remembered how hard it was to get through the day cold turkey, and still said things like, "It's only beer," and "A beer or two won't matter." The truth is, for us, a beer does matter, it's the catalyst to craving something more. Once the alcohol reaches the brain, our inhibitions drop and the desire to use dope overwhelms. I discovered the solution after three years sober, and it was the same one I heard Day 1 in AA -- never take the first drink.

A stubborn drunk, like me, can hear this simple statement, and yet never understand it.

The summer ground along in a predictable fashion. I worked most of the time, spending my free moments with my dear friend Andrea, at her place with Lord Charles, the most spoiled cat in California if not the entire USA. I had taken the camper off the Tundra and slept at the bounce house warehouse on weekends so that I could carry more jumpers and make more money, but it was strange being away from school. The extra money was nice but I often felt like I was wasting time. I would pull up my degree progress report online and see all the big, red squares turning into green circles as the quarters passed. I wanted to be back on campus to hasten that process, and soon my friends' nonsense and Larry, the owner of the bounce house company, convinced me that San Francisco was no longer a place I wanted to be.

I had been hauling jumpers for Larry for two years and was easily his top producer. One day, near the end of the summer, traffic held me up, and one delivery out of seven, was an hour late. The customer refused to pay the full $150 owed for the delivery and gave me $100, "Take it or leave it." I took the money, and when I explained the situation to Larry, I offered to eat half the loss.

Larry became livid. He said he should not have to pay for my mistake, and what if every delivery was $50 short, he would lose a fortune. I pointed out that this was the first delivery in two hundred with a payment issue and that he arranged the delivery schedule, so if time was an issue he could have set it up earlier. As the argument grew more heated, I threw a $50 bill on the floor, and told him to keep the money and shut the fuck up.

After picking up the money, Larry started back pedaling. "It's not about the money," he lied.

I climbed into my truck and drove out of the warehouse doors. I finished out the summer, but when Larry asked me what my plans for next summer were, I told him that because of his asinine behavior they did not include him.

*   *   *

September found me back at school, and the fortunate recipient of a scholarship which enriched me and altered my perspective on life to a far greater extent than the few dollars it added to my bank account.

I had applied to the university general scholarship fund during my initial orientation period a year earlier and one of the requirements was to write an essay explaining why I deserved to be rewarded for my efforts. I wrote a short piece detailing my journey from homelessness to Cal Poly Pomona, submitted it with the necessary forms, and resigned myself to the fact that it would probably not amount to anything.

Deluged with emails at the start of the school year, I received one for the Matt's Run Scholarship. "Geez, they must not know how old I am, I'm not running any 5k," I thought out loud, and sent the email unread to the trash bin.

The next day, I received yet another email from the founders of the run. "Boy, they're really pushing to get people to be a part of this thing," I thought before sending the unread message to internet oblivion.

The following day my phone rang.

"Hello, I'm looking for John McHugh," the voice said.

"You're speaking with John," I answered.

"John, I don't know if I have the right email for you. This is Kelly, I'm calling about the Matt's Run Scholarship."

"God, will these people never stop?" I thought. Keeping my composure, I replied, "Sure what can I do for you?"

"Nothing, just calling to tell you, you won!"

237

I was dumbfounded. "Won what? The scholarship?"

"Yes, you won the $1,000 award. There were nine winners, but you got the Grand Prize."

"I can't believe it," I said. "I don't even remember entering."

"We review the general scholarship applicants, and your essay won. Can you come by for a photo?"

"Sure, just say when. Thank you, thank you so much," I gushed like an Oscar winner.

"We can take the picture this afternoon -- say 2:30 at the Arabian Horse center. Can you make it to campus on Saturday?" Kelly asked.

"I think so," I answered, staring out the window across the parking lot to the starting line of the race.

"Okay, great! On race day just follow the signs that say, 'Award Winners.'"

"Sounds good! See you soon!" I chirped.

My mind raced. A $1,000 given to me by people I had never even met. I had to see what this scholarship was all about and why in the world they would pick me.

Matthew Brent Meyers was a 20-year old junior, majoring in communications at Cal Poly Pomona. Like most young men, he was full of potential, promise and enthusiasm, the world seemingly his for the taking. A tragic twist of fate snatched those hopes away, when, on October 6, 2005, Matt was struck by a car while crossing a street on campus. He died two days later.

From the newspaper accounts, I learned Matt was an avid runner, played guitar, and passionately believed it was his duty to help others less fortunate than himself. Matt left behind his mother, Chris, father, Kevin and sister, Jenna, along with dozens of other family members and friends. Shortly after his death Matt's family began receiving donations from people anxious to help in some way. The money began to add up so they decided around Christmas to do something positive with the accumulated funds. After approaching the university and speaking with President Michael Ortiz, the university added a sizeable donation, and the Matthew Myers Memorial Fund was born.

After meeting his family I gained a much more personal understanding of what, I believe, made Matt so unique. It has been said that tragedy can inspire ordinary people to rise to extraordinary heights and I can think of no better example of this than Kevin, Chris, and Jenna Myers. Losing a child is every parent's worst nightmare, but this family turned their nightmare into a beacon of hope, an act that boggles my mind but inspires and fills my heart as well.

Matt, like me, struggled to get through some of his classes, working hard for the grades he got. His mother explained that someone very close to their family had also found recovery from alcoholism in AA, and the *Readers Digest* version of my own difficulties and subsequent victory over them in my scholarship application touched their hearts and made me an ideal candidate for the award.

The money was wonderful, but as always seems to be the case, it was spent almost as soon as I received it. More significant, I think, are my respect and admiration for the Myers'. They gave me yet another reason to see my dream of a degree through. I couldn't let this wonderful family think their faith in me misplaced. For their kindness, and the confidence they displayed in this drunk from the street, I am eternally grateful.

Today the Matthew Myers Memorial 5K Run is bigger and more festive than ever, with a small army of volunteers, hundreds of runners, joggers, walkers, and stroller pushers enjoying a wonderful day celebrating the life and memory of a young man taken far too soon. Few occasions in my life have made me feel as inspired as winning that award.

* * *

My sophmore year was by far the most difficult of my entire time in school. Along with more and more advanced math classes, the real engineering courses began -- Vector Statistics, Strength of Materials, Fluids, and the mother of them all, Vector Dynamics. I studied day and night but still had to repeat courses to pass. We were given three shots at each course and needed to get a C- or better to move on. Many of my peers were not up to the task and more than a few switched majors to remain in school. I snuck by, barely, taking Strength of Materials to my third strike before squeaking by with a C-.

School occupied every waking hour during most of my second year, but another cool thing happened during the second quarter. Instead of using the school gym to shower every day, my friend and Chemistry lab partner, Natalee, told me about the on-campus health club. Sponsored by the Student Association, it cost only $15 a month to become a member. We started going together on Fridays after class, and within a month I was working out every day. I attacked the gym with an enthusiasm I hadn't felt since my first attempt at college nearly thirty years before. The result of my newfound dedication? I dropped thirty pounds and squeezed back into size 34 pants. For the next six years, I never strayed far from the gym, and made sure to break a sweat at least five days a week which was actually pretty easy because I knew everyone in the place, used the showers every day, and would have been embarrassed to visit the club and not work out.

Between my studies and workouts, the days flew by, but before the year ended, one more tribulation occurred to test both my faith and sobriety. Another grim reminder of where I could end up.

Sammy C had been sleeping in his Ford Explorer by the beach in San Francisco within a hundred yards of where Kelly Harper, the first of my friends to pass, had died.

We talked every evening with Sam getting drunker and drunker until eventually I would say, "Good Night." The conversations were a chore, decidedly one-sided, but Sam was my friend and if he was talking about getting sober then maybe, just maybe, he actually would.

A good portion of our conversations involved him quizzing me about Milano's premature demise. Usually he began or ended with the same question, "I'm not as bad as him, am I?"

He was hoping that I would say, "No Sam, no way," effectively giving him permission to continue drinking. "Well, Sam if you're asking me, you probably already think that you are," was my typical reply.

Another often repeated conversation involved me scolding Sam for drinking and driving. In his defense when you sleep in a vehicle that has to be moved every day, it is next to impossible stay sober long enough to perform the task.

Sam eventually got a drunk driving ticket, but was fortunate enough to not lose the car right away. I tried in vain to persuade him to take his lumps and do the jail time.

"Johnny, I can't do that, I can't take being in jail," he bemoaned every night for a month.

"Sam, just put the car in a garage, or better yet, a storage place. Ask your lawyer, but since it's your first time, and you didn't have an accident, you shouldn't have to do more than a month."

"I don't know, maybe I'll just cut and run," he lamented.

My own history had proven, at least to my mind, that probation was a lost cause. Maybe a month or two in jail would give Sam the sober time he needed to finally pull his life together.

"Look, you'll have two grand in SSI checks waiting for you when you get out. If you want to leave then, great, at least you'll have some running money."

"Yeah, I'll think about it," was the last thing Sammy ever said to me.

His court day came and went without a word, and I thought he had made good on his promise to flee the state until I got a call from Sam's mom, Linda.

"Hi John. The reason I'm calling is I haven't heard from Sam for a week or two, and Sunday was my birthday, and he always calls, even when he was in jail, to wish me Happy Birthday."

"Well, Happy Belated Birthday Linda, but the last time I talked to him was at least a week ago. Linda, let me make some calls to San Francisco and see if anyone up there knows where he is."

"I would really appreciate that, John."

"No problem. I'll call you towards the end of the week."

I ran through the list of usual suspects -- places, programs and people Sam might have turned to in his hour of need. All the leads came up empty, and with my slim hopes fading rapidly I began the miserable task of calling the jails, hospital, and Medical Examiner's office, in that order. It is a sad state of affairs when being incarcerated is the best option but I would have breathed a grateful sigh of relief if Sam was safe and sound locked up in County.

My final call to the ME brought the news I did not want to hear. A body decomposing in the back of a Ford SUV had been found in the parking lot of the La Playa Safeway. Along with the body they found a vial of Percocet, and an open half-gallon bottle of vodka.

"Was the truck a Ford Explorer?" I asked.

"I think so, but without the report in front of me I can't say for sure."

"Listen, it sounds like my buddy. His mom's been calling me, but I'm down in L.A. Could I come up to identify him? His mother is in Texas, near El Paso, but I'd hate to ask her to make the trip. She's got to be eighty."

"Wouldn't work either way," the ME said. "The body is too far gone. It was in the car for two weeks."

I was flabbergasted that his body could remain in the Safeway parking lot that long. "How is that possible?" I asked. If we slept in the woods across the street for more than a couple hours the cops were all over us.

"Hard to say. We have him on video leaving the store with the vodka thirteen days before the smell got so bad that someone finally called it in."

"I guess that rules out foul play?" I asked sarcastically.

"Sure does. Official cause of death is heart failure," the ME answered.

An ignominious end for the Staten Island Viking.

Mother's Day was a week away by the time I got back to Linda. I left out the grisly details and focused instead on the official version of Sam's demise.

"They found a car which matches the one Sam had, down by the beach where we usually stayed." I waited for her to grasp the terrible news I so badly wanted to spare her. "There was a body inside that is most likely Sam's. The medical examiner says the person, a man, died of heart failure."

"Oh, John, "she said in a whisper. "Is there any way to be sure?"

"The ME said they were doing a dental analysis. They have copies of Sam's records now that I gave them his name. The positive identification will take maybe two months."

"Thank you, John," her voice dropped away.

I gave her the name and number for the Medical Examiner.

"Linda, I'm sorry," I blurted out, trying desperately to remain composed. "I loved him too."

"I know, John, we all did."

The receiver clicked, the phone fell silent and I wept for the loss of my friend and for his family.

Linda and I still speak on holidays or when I feel the need to check in and see how she's doing. Even Jenny, Sam's sister, called me out of the blue one night several months later plagued by nightmares of Sam writhing in agony, struggling to escape the confines of the truck, suffocating in the cool foggy night.

I answered the only way I could, with the truth, "Jenny, you know Sam liked pain killers, and of course, any and all types of booze. I think he probably just had some of each, a little too much actually, and drifted off into a pleasant sleep, safe, warm, and secure hidden beneath the blankets in the back of his truck."

"You really think so, John?"

"I know so, Jenny, and no one knew him better than me."

*   *   *

June 2010

Year Two came to an end, and with a lot of work and a little luck, I passed all my classes and managed to keep my GPA at 3.16. I hoped to graduate with something above a 3.0, but as with most transfers, any breathing room I acquired in the less demanding world of community college was disappearing fast. With the most difficult courses behind me, everyone told me things would get better during my junior year, so I put school in my rearview, dropped my truck in the storage area at East Shore, and headed to LAX and a summer in New York.

No longer wanting to return to San Francisco, I had made plans to spend the summer with my family in New York, at my sister's house. My parents would be coming up for a month, and my son wanted to visit too. The relationships I had abandoned were returning to me, and I could not wait to see where this journey would lead.

Mike, a lifelong friend of mine, had begun phoning me in California to ask how I gave up drinking, and turned it all around. I told him to hang in there, I would be home in a week, and I would help him to get straight no matter what the problem was.

I arrived home in mid-June, and after a day or two with my family, hopped in the 1996 Geo Prizm I had repaired, and nicknamed the "Green Meanie" (much to the delight of my younger nephews), and headed to Rogers Lane, the street I grew up on, to see Mike.

"Johnny Boy," Mike growled. "Sure is good to see you."

"Likewise. Tell me what's goin' on with you."

Mike was always big; now he was huge at 6'8" and easily 350 lbs. The last time I had seen him he was playing basketball for Connecticut, just as tall but one hundred pounds lighter.

"I got a problem," he began. "Actually more than just one."

"Come on," I said getting in the Meanie. "Take a ride and you can tell me about it."

Mike plopped into the passenger seat, shifting the entire car with his bulk, and proceeded to talk about all his problems except for his addiction, the root cause of all his other dilemmas. He went on about a breakup he had with the most wonderful girl in the world, family who would not talk to him, spending a few nights in jail due to a driving under the influence ticket, but as always seemed to be the case with people who desperately need to get sober, his biggest worry was money, or more accurately his lack of money.

"All I need is a few grand to set things right, get people off my back, you know?"

A universal belief among addicts, alcoholics, and liberal politicians is, if you throw enough money at a problem, it will magically disappear. Mike was no exception. He believed that if he had enough money, he could fix his life, and still have a little left over to party. The truth is, all the money is dope money, the bills don't get paid, more debt racks up -- in short order, the problems go from bad to worse to insurmountable. Money accelerates this process, it does not slow it down, The only, potentially, good thing, is that it brings you to your knees sooner. Look at John Belushi. In 1978, he was a star on the #1 TV show in the nation, *Live from New York, It's Saturday Night*, starred in the #1 movie, *Animal House*, and had a #1 album, *The Blues Brothers Briefcase Full of Blues*. On March 5, 1982, Belushi died in Bungalow 3 of the Chateau Marmont due to an overdose of heroin and cocaine.

"Mike, you have to put the dope down. All the rest is all because of your using, not the other way around."

"Nah, man, I can put it down, but I still need to get some money together."

"What will that take?" I asked.

Mike had an exterminating business that generated a nice income when running properly. I told him that I wouldn't give him any money, but was willing to work with him for whatever he could pay me.

Because of his DWI conviction, Mike couldn't legally drive, so my main chore was chauffeuring us around in the Prizm. The first few days went well, but on Day 3 his disease reared its ugly head. Mike was fine until about 3 p.m. when, after getting paid for a raccoon removal job, he announced that we needed to stop and pay his Google bill to keep the business in a top Ad Words spot. The idea seemed legit, but as we pulled up to a residence instead of an office, my suspicions grew.

"Mike, why do want to stop here? I thought you had to pay a bill?"

"I am. This is where the guy who set up my Google stuff lives." Mike flung the door open before the car came to a stop, launching his large body faster than I had seen since arriving in New York. "I wouldn't lie to you man! Be out in a second!" he hollered over his shoulder.

Although the house was pristine looking, more like the cover of *Better Homes and Gardens* than a dope house, I held my breath as he disappeared inside.

Mike walked out of the house five minutes later, waving to a well-dressed Indian or Arabic man peeking around the edge of a white screen door. "See? No problems," Mike said as he clambored back into the compact car.

"Where to now?" I asked still giving Mike the once over. He looked perfectly normal, steady gait, eyes clear. No boozy breath or pungent smell of weed.

"Let's go to Robert Moses. I haven't been to the beach in two years."

We were near the Smith Haven Mall on Long Island's north shore. Robert Moses State Park was 15 miles away, a quick ride west along RTE 347, then dead south on the Sagtikos Parkway and Robert Moses Causeway, over the bridges to the beach. The trip would take thirty minutes. Mike seemed fine, and who could argue with a trip to the beach on a beautiful sunny afternoon? I pointed the Meanie west and wound her up to her 65 miles an hour, top speed, a real effort for the little Geo with close to 600 pounds of exterminators in the front seats.

"Hey, Johnny Boy, do you know why the bridges are so low on the parkways?" Mike asked.

I knew I was inviting a history lesson, but I answered, "No man, I have no idea."

Mike's degree was in history, and discussing it, or more accurately lecturing about it, was his passion. He began slowly, building to a fever pitch like an old southern preacher. "Well, see in 1924 Robert Moses took over the development of the roadways. He began developing the plan, but then the depression hit, and he had to wait until Roosevelt started the New Deal in 1933 to start getting the roadways built."

"Teddy or FDR?" I asked. "I can never keep my Roosevelts straight."

"Johnny, FDR was the New Deal," he answered in an exasperated tone.

"So why did they want the bridges so low?"

"That's the fucked up part," Mike continued, his voice and hand movements accentuating the injustice as he spoke. "The New Deal put a lot of people back to work, poor people who began to pay a lot of money in taxes, but Robert Moses didn't want them to be able to use the beaches that their tax dollars and the roads they were building opened up, so they kept the bridges low so buses couldn't fit under them, and only people who had a car could get to them."

"I get it, only rich snobs had cars."

"Yep, so they were the only ones who could use the beaches."

"Makes sense in an elitist sort of way."

"Yeah, except we'd be the ones getting the short end of the stick now."

"Probably," I answered, guiding the car around the cloverleaf entrance to the causeway that bore the tyrant's name.

"Did you know he held his office for over 40 years?" Mike asked.

"Tireless civil servant or despicable bourgeoisie? The world may never know," I added.

"Oh, Johnny, we know, we know for sure."

The discussion reminded me of many we had shared in days gone by, Mike pontificating, me trying to goad him into an argument. We reached the beach and parked in a lot just after the toll collectors closed their doors.

"Johnny, I've got to take a leak," Mike said and headed off towards the large open-air restroom.

I stayed behind basking in the sun. About ten minutes later he reappeared on the boardwalk and began walking towards me. Out of my sight for mere minutes, he was obviously not the same guy when he reached me. He

250

began to speak, but his words were muffled and slurred, a little at first, but soon I couldn't understand him at all.

"Come on," I ordered, and headed for the car. I knew he had taken something, something he had gotten during our stop to "Pay the bill."

He slumped into the seat, and began nodding off as I started the car, and drove out of the lot. By the time we were back on the parkway I was worried he would OD right then and there. I had no idea what or how much dope he had taken, and his behavior was growing worse by the minute. It was like he had managed to get falling down drunk in the blink of an eye. I wondered how bad he would get before it killed him.

Just as I was about to head for the hospital, Mike put his seat back, and dropped into a deep sleep, loud grating snores bellowing from his monstrous frame. Once back on the north side of the Island, I parked at a shopping center and debated what my next move should be.

I could dump him at his mom's house, where he was staying, but I didn't know if she had ever seen him like this. The hospital was still an option -- Saint Catherine's was only a few minutes away. My third option was to wait it out, and see if he came around. With his breathing steady and strong, I figured time was on my side so I bought a newspaper and some food to weather the storm. Occasionally Mike would wake up, say something unintelligible, then pass back out, or play with the heater controls and cigarette lighter trying to turn the radio on. I waited, wondering how this could possibly be called getting high, when it looked like no fun at all.

Two hours later, Mike began to make some sense; he started looking around in a slow, bewildered way, and asked, "Where the hell are we?"

"In Commack, by the diner," I told him. "What the fuck did you take?"

"Nothing," he answered. "I'm just tired."

"Bullshit, Mike! You were so fucked up, I was heading to the hospital to get your stomach pumped!"

"It was just a couple Oxies," he said. "I'm sorry, man."

"Don't tell me you're sorry, and don't tell me you wouldn't lie to me. You don't give a shit about me, and you would lie to Jesus Christ himself to get your fuckin' fix."

"I don't do needles," he said.

"Sure you do. Maybe not today, but in a day or two, you'll be happy to stick yourself to get high. I've seen guys so hard up for dope they would rob someone, buy whatever shit they could, then rinse their rig in a puddle to shoot up."

"What do you want me to do?" Mike shouted. "Don't try that tough love stuff, that doesn't work on me, I need someone to help me!"

"No, you don't. You want someone to drive you around, do your jobs for you so you can get paid, and run to the dope man. I want you to stop right now, cold turkey. If you can't do that ,you need more than I can give you, maybe an inpatient detox, then a program."

"What the fuck, man? I just got out of prison, and now you want to lock me up again?"

My blood really began to boil. This fuckin' 6'8" candy-ass pussy had no idea how bad things could get. "You call a month, no 21 days, being locked up? Forty years old and you run back to your mama, only to spit in her face, mooching off her, pretending to work just so you can get high!"

"What the fuck, man? I don't need this!"

I heard the quiver in his voice and continued my attack. They say never kick a man when he's down, but with dope fiends and boozers you must strike when they are vulnerable and desperate if there is any chance of the words getting through. Few people walk willingly through the doors of recovery. Most crawl.

"No, you do need this, this is exactly what you fuckin' need," I bellowed. "Here's how it's going to go. You empty your pockets right now, and if you use again, I am gone, and I guarantee you will be dead within a year."

"I can't quit cold turkey," Mike said. "I need a little just to stay well."

The cat was out of the bag. Mike was using all day, every day. He was right, he might not be able to stop on his own now. Though I wasn't completely familiar with the differences between drug addiction and alcoholism, I realized that Mike was attempting to maintain -- using just enough to get by; that's why he got so messed up so quickly, and why the drugs seemed to wear off so fast.

"Well, then you'll have to get in a program, inpatient, outpatient, methadone clinic, I don't care, but I'm not going to sit here, and watch you, no, help you die. I've done that before, and it sucks, it really sucks."

"Well, it will be hard, but I can try. How about if I just smoke a little weed to get over the rough spots?"

Normally I would not have agreed to even this, but sometimes you take what you can get, and in reality, I had no control over what Mike did.

"I guess so. We can work on the weed later, but if this happens again you go straight to an inpatient program for a month, three months, six months whatever they tell you. I'm going to find out who would even take your sorry ass. Deal?"

"Yeah, Johnny, deal, just don't leave me."

253

"I will stay as long as you need me, you have my word on that, but if you continue to use then my help is not enough for you, and you'll have to find another way. Or not. Believe me, dying is always an option."

Mike nodded his head yes with tears rolling down his face. I reached over and hugged him though both my arms could not reach around his huge body.

"It's going to be really hard," he said.

"Yes, but you can do it," I answered, switching from bad cop to cheerleader.

Mike remained true to his word, although the weed smoking definitely increased. To my knowledge he stopped using opiates that day. Initially I would get hourly reports on how bad it was. Nausea, vomiting, aches, and pains, almost exactly like having the flu. This is the hump many addicts can't get over; they use again, just a little, to get well, but a little turns into a little more, a little more becomes a lot more, and the cycle begins again. Addiction is sadistic, torturing the user with the knowledge that the cure to all that ails them is simply doing some more.

A week of constant monitoring passed, and Mike seemed to be past the physical part of his withdrawal. He was more like the old Mike I loved, laughing a lot, eating a lot more – god, could he eat! The business began picking up too, as the Ad Words money was actually going to Google. I would check each day, and we were consistently in the top three slots.

We reminisced constantly about growing up together. Since I was ten years older than Mike, our earliest memories were quite different -- he was the little kid, I was the older buddy.

When Mike was a senior in high school we really hit it off. He came to work for me along with his cousin, Matt, as laborers. I would do my best to make sure these two greenhorns got a taste of what it was like to really work. On the road at 5 a.m., 8 hours in the summertime heat and humidity of New York City, then fight the traffic home to Smithtown, 46 miles east. Mike would stumble up the steps, swearing he was done for the night, but I knew his weakness, his Achilles' heel, and I would go around back to the basketball court.

I would pick up the basketball and start dribbling, "thwack, thwack, thwack, thawk, thwack." Then I would launch a 3-pointer; if I missed, it would clang loudly off the rim, shaking the chain net beneath. If I hit the shot clean, it was just the swish of the chains. Sometimes I got lucky, and the ball bounced around before it fell through, two for the price of one.

Mike's voice would plead from the window above, muffled because the side of his face was mashed in a pillow, "Not tonight, John, I'm too tired."

Sometimes I would keep dribbling and shooting, maybe letting a distinctive Marv Albert "YESSS and it counts!" go after a swish; other times I would take a more direct approach.

"No, don't get up. You stay there. I'll just tell everybody that you were afraid to face me tomorrow."

Or I'd play the age card. "This is so sad. Nineteen years old, and you can't keep up with an old man like me!".

Like Poe's Tell-Tale Heart, the pounding of the ball on the pavement driving him insane, I would hear the creak of the wooden screen door and Mike would appear, staring down from the raised wooden deck above. The game was on.

He would destroy me. I could barely touch the rim with a running jump. He could touch it by raising his hand. He would back me down to one spot where a golden pebble poked through the concrete court, then launch a Kareem-

255

style sky hook I had no defense against. I would run around like a chicken without a head, scrambling for every loose ball, going left, going right, raining down half court shots. If I was lucky, I lost only 21 to 16. We would play until the light was gone, sometimes turning on the one floodlight so he could pile on a few more points.

"Why do you always do this, when you know I am going to kick your ass?" Mike would ask.

"Keeps me on my toes. Besides I'll get even at work tomorrow," I would reply.

The Google Ads worked too well and soon we had more work then we could handle. More customers meant more money, but also more jobs to finish. I would pick Mike up at 8:00 a.m. every day and we never finished before 6:00 p.m., seven days a week. It was a good thing for his recovery, as well as his wallet, leaving him little time to screw up.

One night, after finishing our last job, we stopped at Home Depot across from Syosset Hospital to pick up a roll of wire mesh to rat-proof a crawl space the next day.

"Did you know I was born in that hospital?" Mike asked.

"Of course I do, I was there." I answered.

"No you weren't." he replied.

"I most certainly was! My mom packed all your family and mine, eight of us kids, into our old Dodge wagon to come see Karen's new baby. We weren't supposed to be allowed in, but the nurses let us all sneak down the hall to the nursery window to take a peak. You were supposed to be 14 to visit. I was only 10 so it was a big thrill."

"Wow," said Mike. "We've known each other my entire life."

"Yes we have," I replied. " And that means you buy dinner, boss."

The summer was rolling along quite nicely when my mom asked me to take her and Dad to visit her sister, my Aunt Margaret, in Ozone Park. It was only one Sunday, but still I worried about Mike, so I asked him before saying OK.

"Mike, man, I'm thinking about taking Sunday off. I have to take my parents into the City. Are you going to be alright with that?"

Mike put on his blustery, confident face, and accompanying deep voice. "Sure, Johnny. Nothing to worry about. I could use a day off too."

"Look, you have a lot of money, and it's hasn't even been two months. Sure you can handle it?"

"What? The dope? Why? I don't even miss it," he lied.

I knew it was a lie because at two months sober you probably spend 70% of your waking hours thinking about using.

"Alright, It's only for the one day. I'll be back bright and early Monday."

Mike and I parted with a hug and a warning. "Any problem, just call me. My phone is on all the time."

The trip to Ozone Park went without incident. My aunt was delighted to see us and we spent the afternoon at her favorite diner on Rockaway Boulevard.

Bright and early Monday morning I called Mike to see what was on the agenda for the day. His phone went straight to voicemail, a bad sign right out of the gate

I called the house phone, and again, after twenty rings, still no answer. Bad sign number two.

I hopped in the Green Meanie and drove to the house. After banging loudly failed to bring anyone to the door I made my way to the backyard. The smell of weed wafted over the high picket fence before I even opened the gate. Mike sat beside the basketball court on a white painted wicker chair, smoking from an aluminum beer can he had dented, and poked a hole in to use as his pipe. At first I felt relieved -- maybe Mike was just smoking some weed when I called before, but all my hopes faded when he spoke. He slurred like his brain was operating at about a quarter its normal speed. "Johnny Boy," he growled, slowly extending the pipe to me with his long arm. "Have some, you know you want to."

The time for yelling was over. "No Mike, I don't want any. Guess we're not working today." I turned and walked out the gate. Mike followed, banging along the side of the house, lunging past me to grab the passenger door.

"No, don't be mad. You want to work, let's go. I can work, I can work right now." He pulled the door open and dropped into the seat, banging the back of his head on the doorframe before pulling his legs in.

"No, I don't feel like working. I'll come back tomorrow," I said, tears filling my eyes. I didn't want to cry, didn't want to show any sign of weakness, but this was too much. I could not hold the emotions in as hard as I tried.

"What? What's the matter? Johnny, I just had a little, only three Oxies, that's nothing man."

I didn't yell. I couldn't, my voice cracked as I plead with him, "You just don't get it Mike, this shit will kill you, and if you don't stop you will be dead, sooner not later."

"John, it was over a month. I needed a little break. We were working all the time, I just needed a little break."

"Look, I'll be back tomorrow," I said formulating a plan before starting the car.

"Tomorrow, I'll be ready. Tomorrow, right?"

"Yeah," I said, and he hugged me so hard I could barely breathe.

My first stop was the Apple Rehabilitation Center on Veterans Highway in Hauppauge near my sister's house.

258

Pulling to a gate, complete with a guard, I asked for permission to enter the facility. "Hey guy, my buddy is having a hard time. He's using opiates a lot, and I was hoping to talk to a counselor or something."

"Well, I can't just let you in. You need an appointment, and someone will come out, and meet you," the gatekeeper answered.

"Okay, sounds fair," I replied. I knew the man working the gate was most likely a current or former client, so I quickly added, "How could he get in? Is it hard?"

He thought for a minute, then told me what he knew about the admission process. "Well, you can't be using, not at all. They test you before letting you in. The easiest way is to come in through a detox. They'll still test you, but you will know you're going to be clean."

"Any suggestions, places I could try for a detox?"

"I've been clean for three years. The place I went to closed down a year or so ago. Maybe try the Salvation Army, they have detoxes you know."

I smiled a little, drifting back to my own struggles a few years before. "Yeah I know the place. Thank you."

At my sister's house I combed the internet looking for a detox that would take Mike. I made a list of the names and numbers of three good options, placed it in the glove compartment of the Geo, and joined my family for dinner.

I slept well. I had a plan for a one-man intervention, and the information needed to carry it out. I would get Mike to a detox, then try to explain to his family that bailing him out with food, money and a place to live enabled him to keep using and squandering his earnings on dope. Next I would meet with a counselor at Apple, hopefully with Karen, Mike's mom. His only remaining option would be to give the rehab a try. All I had to do was persuade Mike to say yes. As with any intervention, the

259

addict has to agree, even if they have a litany of reservations ;they have to be the one to say, "OK, I'll do it."

I tried Mike's phone about 9:00 a.m. not worried about the late start as I had no intention of going to work. The phone rang and rang.

I tried again after 10. For a second time, no answer.

I called the house phone, the number embedded in my brain after dialing it for the past 35 years. "Hello?" a woman's voice answered. It was Michelle, Mike's sister.

"Hey, Michelle, it's John. Is Mike there? He isn't answering his phone, and I was hoping we were working today."

"Hi John. I'll go get him, he isn't up yet," she replied.

I heard her set down the phone, and waited an uncomfortably long time before Michelle's voice returned to the line, gasping, "John, he's dead, oh my God, he's dead!"

"Michelle, dead to the world or dead, dead?"

She kept screaming, "No, John, DEAD! He's not moving, not breathing, oh ,my God! What do I do?"

"Call an ambulance!" I shouted, running to the car. "Michelle," I asked, fumbling with the phone as I drove. "Did you call them? Did you get an ambulance?"

"Yes, John, they just got here, they're in with him now."

"Hang on, I'm on Ridge Road, I'll be there in two minutes."

"Hurry," was all she said.

The scene outside the house was the organized mayhem typical of an emergency response -- an ambulance backed into the driveway, a fire truck, lights flashing, motor idling with a pair of firefighters standing beside it, I jumped from the car and ran up the steps as another fireman came out of the house.

"Who are you?" he asked.

"Mike's friend, John," I answered. "We've been working together."

Michelle's voiced called from behind the firefighter, "That's John. Let him in. Is he dead? Is he going to be OK?"

The fireman lowered his eyes, and shook his head. Michelle shrieked from behind me in the kitchen. "Can you give us a hand?" he asked, waving to his two men to join us.

"Sure," I answered, and followed him up the hallway.

Surreal does not begin to describe the scene in Mike's bedroom. Two paramedics were packing their gear, while a huge body bag stuffed with Mike's remains lay on the king-sized bed in the center of the room, his frame so large, his Size 13 feet stuck through the zipper at the end of the bag. "Grab hold," the firefighter said. I reached for a handle near his head, not wanting to stare down at Mike's bizarrely protruding feet.

Even with six men moving Mike's immense body through the narrow hallway and down the stairs proved to be a daunting task.

Michelle emerged from the kitchen, and for the first time I saw Karen, Mike's mom, tears streaming down her face as she clutched her daughter in grief. We descended to the truck below, and at the bottom of the concrete porch steps, we placed the body atop the ambulance gurney to lift it inside.

"Wait, wait!" Michelle cried, running from the house clutching a vial of holy water. She poured the bottle over Mike as the firemen and I paused. Michelle prayed, Karen prayed, I prayed, and I think a few of the others probably joined in as well; if not, they were kind enough to give us a few minutes to say goodbye.

Soon after Mike's body was loaded into the ambulance, the house began to fill with family and friends coming to offer whatever comfort they could. The police asked many questions hoping to find out where Mike had gotten the dope from. I told them about the house, I told them about other situations that just didn't add up. At one point a detective asked if I would be willing to be a part of their investigation.

"Without a doubt," I replied.

The funeral was a sad, sad affair. Mike was laid out at the front of the room, a snug fit inside the confines of the tufted coffin. In death he looked quite like he had in life, at least the last time I had talked with him, the only obvious difference being the lack of sparkle normally visible in his now sewn shut eyes.

A small controversy brewed from Michelle's desire to place a shiny, horned Viking helmet on Mike's head. Apparently Mike had enjoyed some celebrity on a cable TV reality fishing show in which he was known as Olaf the Viking. The rest of the family felt it was not appropriate for the somber occasion and vetoed the idea, but Michelle, never a girl to quietly concede anything, lobbied for the helmet continuously throughout the first day of visitation.

Beside the coffin was a picture of Mike in far better days. He was in game shape, fresh from a season at Connecticut, his shoulder length blonde hair lightened by the strong Florida sun. He really did look like a Viking, towering above the crowd, broad shoulders, trim waist, flowing hair, all of it reinforcing Michelle's side of the helmet argument. Time and his hard living had taken its toll -- a Viking helmet on the modern day, bloated version of Olaf, impropriety aside, would have just looked silly.

Along one wall of the chapel stood a collection of photographs taken throughout Mike's life. I was in several, along with many of the people with whom we had grown up, some of them now standing in the chapel that very day. It broke my heart to see how many friends and family members Mike had left behind.

When the Bob, Pete, Sam and my other friends had died, my involvement with the family had been limited to a prayer that they rest in peace, a few hours in the funeral parlor, or in Sammy's case, a dozen phone calls to assist and comfort his mom. With Mike, my emotions were deep, intense, and personal.

They were all my friends, some among my best, but I hadn't grown up with them -- talking, playing, crying, and laughing with them as the years went by. I did not have their mothers weeping on my shoulder, their brothers asking, "What else could we have done?"

As I made the rounds of the funeral hall the attendees expressed dismay, sadness, disillusionment, maybe a little disappointment, but no one was angry. They all wondered how someone so much larger than life, in every sense of the word, could be gone so quickly, for no apparent reason.

My self-centered thoughts turned to my own not-so-distant past and I realized that I could easily be in that box instead of Mike. Any of a dozen predicaments I managed to wriggle out of during the last 10 years could have punched my ticket and removed me from the game for good. My mother would have been the one weeping in my sisters' arms, my family asking why? Though I imagine my end would have been more like Sammy's, with one of the gardeners discovering my decomposing corpse hidden among the bushes in Golden Gate Park or washed up at Ocean Beach.

It was the first time that I realized, deep down, that my behavior, my choices, caused others great pain. Simply not being around every day did not absolve me of my responsibility to, at least, try to live something resembling a normal life.

Alcoholics and addicts typically believe that they, *we*, are worthless; therefore our families and friends cannot actually care about us. This belief manifests itself in two different behaviors. One, we leave, sure that the grass is greener anywhere but where we are standing, and, since we are nothing but burdens to those who love us, we will not be missed. More extreme, we believe that they'll say, "Good riddance," and thus we can go on destroying our lives with a little less guilt. Two, we become angry, blaming the people we love for our own shortcomings. The result is the same -- we alienate those we care about, and who care about us, giving ourselves permission to continue drinking and using.

Casting off these anchoring relationships, our only tethers to the fleeting threads of reality, allows us to drift further away, to fall deeper through the cracks, until, at last, we become the filthy, sun-scorched faces and shivering skeletons that crawl into the daylight to hunt through trash cans for food, or beg for change along highway ramps.

I am guilty of employing both of these tactics in my own life, deluding myself, and attempting to dupe others, into believing that my actions were anything but selfish. I was being considerate, noble in fact, leaving my family and friends alone to live their productive lives. The fact is my absence tortured them, while allowing me to do whatever I wanted without regard to consequences or guilt.

"I am not hurting anyone but myself, "and, "I didn't ask you to care," become the battle cries when the people who love you beg you to stop.

I stayed at the funeral home throughout both visitation days, sat beside my parents for Mike's last Mass, and accompanied the parade of headlights following the long black hearse to a little cemetery on the far side of town. The gravesite sat adjacent to a condo development, that had been the Yellow Top Farm where I worked as a teenager.

One by one the cars parked along the twisting cemetery drive. The women touched up their makeup in rearview mirrors, and the men stood alongside driver's doors pulling on dark suit jackets, before beginning the climb to the top of the green hillside. A huge clay mound flanked the open grave, the dark brown soil bleached dry, nearly white, on its edges in the midday sun. The casket had been delivered via mechanical lift before the group arrived, sparing the pallbearers the possible hernias associated with lugging 500 pounds across 600 feet of cemetery.

The preacher spoke, some prayers were recited as heads bowed and tears fell from beneath dark glasses. Then each mourner filed passed the coffin, taking one last look while leaving a flower to say goodbye. Thankfully the coffin remained above ground until well after everyone was gone, saving the family the anguish of seeing Mike descend into the unforgiving earth. Another friend was gone, but I now had another angel watching over me.

*   *   *

During my junior year the focus of my classes shifted from learning the material and methods of engineering to applying them to real world problems. Though the classroom situations were somewhat contrived, they provided good practice using problem solving techniques. At this point I actually began enjoying the classes, not just the relationships with fellow students and teachers.

My computer skills grew exponentially. I was using a dozen different software programs to solve a myriad of different engineering challenges, from modeling building frames in SAP2000 to highway design in Bentley Inroads. I began tracking my degree progress report in earnest, no longer content to sit back and count the green circles. I needed to formulate an exit strategy, so I chose an option in Geo-Spatial Engineering and began the downhill run.

Not only did my course schedule change, but my attitude and self-confidence did as well. I became absorbed in the day-to-day machinations of passing classes and achieving a degree that I began to forget my past -- a good and bad thing -- as letting the past go is necessary to move forward but forgetting it condemns one to repeat it.

A chance discussion on one of my favorite radio shows brought a new perspective to my achievements thus far. I have always been a sports radio junkie, the neverending banter between the hosts and callers soothes me, reminding me of when I worked as a bartender at TJ Markum's Irish Pub in New York. The patrons would argue ad infinitum, nearly coming to blows over the most inane, insignificant topics, using any excuse to start an argument disguised as conversation.

While in San Francisco I began listening to Sports Radio 680 KNBR. It soon became my favorite way to pass the hours whether working or studying. One particular Thursday afternoon I was listening, via the miracle of internet streaming, to The Razor and Mr. T Show. Tom Tolbert, retired NBA journeyman turned talk radio star, was relaying an effort by the city of Seattle to give away booze, to his intelligent, articulate, if somewhat long-winded co-host, Ralph Barbieri.

Apparently Seattle's political brain trust had proposed providing free alcohol to its chronic alcoholics to prevent them from drinking mouthwash and hand sanitizer, like the Sterno bums of the 1930's, indigents who strained the flammable jelly through cheesecloth to extract the alcohol. Research had shown that it would be cheaper to give the boozehounds free drinks, than to pay for hospital costs and mortuary expenses. This coldly logical system possessed a sort of benign, pseudo-Nazi efficiency, giving new meaning to the term "assisted suicide," as the government would not only assist, but foot the bill as well.

Alcoholics who drink for free will do so until they are dead. Treatment, however, is costly, lengthy, and often futile, so perhaps it is better for all involved to shorten the path from cradle to grave, greasing the skids to remove this financial burden from society. Which sounds reasonable until it is your loved one, your son, daughter, sister, brother, or parent, caught in the grips of addiction.

As their conversation continued I became aware that had I been fortunate enough to not have any of my coronary problems, I would probably be heading north to the Promised Land for the free booze, hoping to kick a hand sanitizer habit. See, when you drink the way that I had, achievements are measured by what you have not done *yet*. It's part of the "I'm not as bad as the next guy rationalization of every miserable choice of your life. I would not have awakened one morning consumed with the notion of drinking hand sanitizer or slowly warmed to the idea after careful consideration. "I have a great idea! Instead of getting a bottle today, I'll get a quart of hand sanitizer! It's much cheaper and has the same effect!"

A more plausible scenario would be waking up broke, mind racing, consumed with the DT's and someone suggesting drinking a few shots of sanitizer. "It's not that bad, worked for me," they would tempt.

"Give it to me," would have been my response as yet another line was crossed.

At that moment I began to savor the enormity of the changes in my life. Prior to stopping drinking, for what I pray is the last time, I had guzzled Listerine with a few friends in the Golden Gate Park Panhandle because that was all we had.

Six years later, and here I am, sequestered in the Cal Poly University Library analyzing the structural integrity of building frames, understanding and applying levels of physics and mathematics I barely knew existed – blessed in so many ways simply because I stopped drinking.

This realization is both astounding and humbling. Astounding because, in my wildest dreams, I could never have imagined the sense of purpose, accomplishment and gratitude I feel now, and humbling because I still can't believe I allowed myself to sink to such depths of misery and despair. Still, I am never angry that it happened, that I was so weak, because these very same failures forced me to grow.

I often joke with my mom that all my years of drinking were necessary because my mind was too powerful – I had to destroy several billion brain cells before I could handle its immense capabilities. Truth be told, it took all these years of sobriety to begin to understand what a wonder the human mind is.

* * *

As the first quarter of my Junior year came to a close, I returned to New York to spend the holidays with my family on Long Island, a dicey proposition at best, with so many memories, good and bad, triggered by the people and places I hadn't seen in years. I had the persistent feeling that although Long Island was special, it no longer was where I belonged. To quote Neil Diamond, "L.A.'s fine, but it ain't home, New York's home but it ain't mine no more."

On this particular trip, as I drove past my old haunts, my mind drifted back to just after high school, and a young woman still near and dear to my heart. As I found my way in sobriety, there were moments when I misconstrued the promises of AA, along with the very principles keeping me sober, as signs from heaven that something I wanted was indeed God's will, and not some selfish desire my brain was telling me I couldn't live without. Such was the case with the search, my foray in trying to recapture my past.

The initial impetus for the search came as I traveled through New York City to my buddy, Mark's, house in Hartsdale. It was mid-December, and the fading daylight and sharp winds turned a brilliant winter day into an icy, ear-biting torment. I abandoned my short walk north to Times Square, ducking down the steps to the 6th Avenue subways into a funky, but welcome, blast of warm, humid air, produced by throngs of commuters scurrying through Pennsylvania Station below.

With my back pressed against a ceramic tiled wall on the northbound platform whose bright white grout had been transformed into a pasty almond by decades of passing trains, my eyes drifted lazily, vacantly, as I waited for the Uptown Number One to arrive. I noticed a couple waiting nearby, conspicuous in the bleak tunnel because of their attire. The man, dashing and debonair, wore a black tux and held a violin case in the crook of his left arm, reminding me of old movies where an impeccably dressed John Dillinger-type would fling open his case to reveal a Thompson sub machine gun killing everyone in sight.

Beside him stood a stunning blonde woman, resplendent in a red satin gown. her shoulders wrapped in chinchilla, wearing a jeweled necklace that would have been at home behind the glass at Tiffany and Co. The radiant stones nestled perfectly between her sweeping neck and ample breasts. She seemed oddly familiar.

While intently watching the pair, so incongruous in the soot-laden tunnel, a thought percolated in my brain. Years, no decades before, I had said goodbye to a similar woman not that far from this very spot. "Could it possibly be her?"

The train roared into the station as I leaned forward straining to hear a note of familiarity in her voice. An instant before shrugging off the encounter and the thought of a reunion, I turned to steal one last glance. She reached to her right, and lifted a black cello case from behind the edge of the wooden bench. It had to be her.

We had not seen each other or spoken in nearly 20 years, but Laura was my Barringer Meteor Crater, embedded forever in my mind.

Things had not ended badly; to my mind at least, they had never officially ended. There had never been a final goodbye and good riddance, no door slamming exits or tear-stained faces watching ships sail from piers. I always felt there might be a chance to somehow rekindle the past. The last time we met proved to be awkward at best, ending with her scolding me for drunken phone calls made to win her back. Her words bounced off my thick head, but their meaning, the very caring and concern I so desperately sought, flew far above it.

Today, I assuage my battered self-esteem with the thought that there may have been a chance, however slight, had I not waited another two decades to turn my life around. Back then, I was too self-absorbed, riddled with guilt and shame, to recognize her attempt to save me. Her passionate beseeching fell on deaf and bitter ears. I walked away, consumed with self-loathing, having blown my golden opportunity, because I wanted to drink even more than I wanted her.

I heard rumors over the years, the grapevine offering a myriad of possibilities as to Laura's fate. She was married, or not. She had given up her dreams of sitting first chair, or she was playing with the symphony at Carnegie Hall. She worked every job from waiting tables in an all-night diner to producing cable TV. As time passed, I conjured up my own fables until I couldn't differentiate between what I had been told and what I imagined. But that day, waiting on that subway, felt like a second chance at redemption, the Ninth Step Promises coming true, fate interceding to grant me one last shot at the impossible dream if only it was indeed her, first loves are that powerful. They shape us, magnifying every experience tenfold, not only because they are new, but because they are shared with someone so special.

A day never passes that I don't think of her and smile. I still recall fondly the first time we met, the first time I held her in my arms, the first time she said, "I love you," and really meant it.

Laura gave me a small, silver cross the first Christmas we shared, explaining that it wasn't gold, therefore not gaudy, nor too big, thus not preachy -- it was like the baby bear's bed, just right. I thought it was perfect, like her.

We went down the street to a neighbor's house for an after-Christmas/pre-New Year's bash, and the next day I awoke to find the silver cross no longer around my neck. I searched the bed, my room, my car, everywhere to no avail. The perfect little cross was gone.

I was crestfallen. What could I possibly tell her? That I had lost the first gift she had given me in less than 24 hours? One month into my 18th year, my life had ended. I dressed and drove to Laura's house bracing myself for the worst. My despair must have been evident the moment she saw me, because when I confessed my carelessness to her, Laura slid into her coat and boots. "Let's go find it," she whispered to me, softly kissing my neck.

The idea was ludicrous, there was a foot of snow on the ground the day before, and nearly another had fallen during the night; but off we went, trudging down the street, a shovel in my left hand, her hand held tightly in my right. Arriving at the house, I dug through the snow like a man possessed, the neighbors delighting in the fact that Laura's crazy boyfriend was kind enough to clear their walk. An hour passed, then two. My trench neared the edge of the street where the snowplows had passed several times, but there was still no sign of the cross.

*Then following one particularly large shovelful, Laura
tugged my sleeve, her fair skin and blonde hair in stark
contrast to her cherubic cheeks flushed red from the cold,
and pointed to the mound I had been creating. "What's
that?" she asked.*

*There, in the snow, a small glint of silver danced in the
rays of the setting winter sun. The perfect little cross was
saved. She picked it up and draped it around my neck. I
held it up for a closer look and realized it was marred, no
longer perfect. The cross had been nicked by the shovel
and gouged down one side. "It's ruined," I blurted out.*

*She looked closely, studying the damage intently, and
with all the wisdom amassed in her 15 years said, "No
Johnny, lines of character." Thirty years later, if my truck
gets a scratch, I whisper, "Lines of character," to myself,
and my heart squeezes a little tight in my chest.*

The pair stepped aboard the train as I slipped inside
the closing doors. I still said nothing, trying to roll back the
years in my mind, searching for one more clue that would
tell me unequivocally that the woman with the cello was
Laura. My stop came too quickly, and I left the train
without ever really knowing, but it made no difference,
the seed of the search had been planted.

Over the next several days I searched the Internet for
information, shunning the more intrusive "pay for
information" services, and concentrating on social
networking sites, which I deemed to be fair game, since
anyone who put information out there must not mind
being "found." On MySpace, I finally found what I had
been looking for: her name, address, date of birth, and
workplace, all confirmed the most accurate rumors. Best
of all, her relationship status listed her as single.

I carefully composed an email to break the ice after two decades. I waited until I returned to California to send it so as to not appear to be the stalker I was quickly becoming. She never replied, and each time I returned to New York I would wonder why. Had my behavior years before offended her so deeply she vowed never to speak with me again? Had the news of my alcoholism and its consequences spanned this great nation to confirm what she had suspected years before? Had she followed what seemed to be a growing trend, and become a lesbian who wanted nothing to do with men? I prayed for answers.

A year and a half later, while spending another summer with my family in New York, I drove past the house Laura had grown up in for the fiftieth time, hoping to catch a glimpse of her, and right out front were her mom and dad. The years had been kind to them; approaching 80, they looked remarkably as I had remembered them. I guess my eyes and memories had aged at the same rate as they had. They were tending to the lawn and garden, that I recalled her father meticulously maintained. Unable to contain my curiosity, I stopped and walked cautiously towards them.

"Hello, remember me?" I asked. There was a hint of recognition in both their faces. "John," I nudged. As I said my name, the floodgates opened. "John McHugh," her mother said. "How have you been?"

We talked for a while about careers, retirement, how great everyone looked, how funny life is, until I finally asked about "the girls," Laura and her sister, Allison. I quickly learned what they had been up to the past 30 years.

Both were ,moms themselves now, living in a neighboring state. As to the all-important question, Laura was married, happily, with two little girls of her own. We talked a bit longer and I said goodbye with a shake of her dad's hand, and a peck on her mom's cheek, something I don't think I had ever done before.

Driving away, a strange contentment swept over me. Surprisingly, I wasn't disappointed at all, instead I felt happy, truly happy, deep down inside that the girl I held so dear, was now a woman, safe, warm, and loved by her husband and two little girls. There was no jealousy, no "could have or should have been me" sentiment, only great joy in knowing that things had apparently gone well in her life. It was then that I realized I must have really loved her for all those years, because all selfish feelings ceased to exist when exposed to the light of her truth.

Perhaps those few years with Laura, so long ago, had etched some "lines of character" on my heart as well.

* * *

January 2011

The 2nd quarter of the school year 2011 always seemed endless. In New York this could be attributed to the freezing weather that made venturing outside anytime from January to early March a chore. In Southern California, where each day is more beautiful than the next, and switching from skiing to surfing can be accomplished with a two-hour drive, you would think that feeling wouldn't exist, but the quarter drags on until the Ides of March make way for Spring Break.

When I arrived at Cal Poly back in September 2008 I phoned my cousin, Elizabeth, my only relative west of the Mississippi, to tell her I had relocated from San Francisco to Los Angeles. Elizabeth had moved from Scotland to Los Angeles eighteen years earlier, and was now the co-owner of a successful hair salon, The Lounge, located in Westwood beside the UCLA campus. We had promised to meet up sometime in the very near future but, as often happens, that day had fallen into the "someday soon" category.

My memories of Elizabeth were comprised mainly of a blonde, cute-as-a-button six-year old pounding out the same song over and over on the piano while visiting at my mom's. Finally, her older brother, Tom, would holler, "Elizabeth! Stop it!" His strong Scottish brogue amused me and my brother, Paul to no end, so much so, we still imitate it today.

When Maddie and I finally met up it was for the christening of her first born, a beautiful baby girl, born in early May, named Maddie. Following a nasty divorce soon after, Elizabeth and Maddie became integral parts of my life. Although we would only see each other a few times each month, a bond developed as I watched this little bundle of joy grow. Now approaching four, she is the precocious little lady who calls me Uncle John.

Up until Maddie came along the bulk of my experience with young children had been with boys, mainly my son and six nephews, but Miss Maddie and I share a unique bond forged in the silliness a grown man can only display with a trusted little girl. With boys everything is silly -- most don't breathe a serious breath until they are walking down the aisle. Little girls, as I quickly discovered, are quite serious about a lot of things at a very young age. They are serious about their clothes, their hair, their story time, their Hello Kitty dresses and they are very, very serious about Disney Princesses.

I don't know how it happened -- I mean I was standing right there and I didn't even see it -- but one day we jumped from Curious George to a litany of daring young heroines who sang, swam, danced, and froze their way into our lives. Every car ride was accompanied by Ariel's operatic *Part of Your World*, her voice so sweet a sea witch swindled it from her in exchange for a pair of legs. Every visit included a showing of Netflix's latest princess offering. Boxes of small statuettes appeared, growing with each release or re-release of a full-length motion picture. The apartment was full of Disney royalty, but to my mind, there was only one real princess, Miss Maddie herself.

At the park one hot day, when Miss M grew tired of leaping from the swings to the monkey bars, we retired to a concrete picnic table in the shade of a eucalyptus tree. Occupying the mind of a four-year old for one last hour before her mother arrives is no easy task, but I had an ace in the hole, or more accurately, a bag of peanut M&M's in my pocket.

"Are they for me?" she asked, spying the bright yellow bag as I slowly drew it from my pocket.

"Yes, but these are so good, so wonderful, I can't just give them away," I answered. "So let's play a game."

"What game?"

"I don't know, we can just make it up."

"We can't make up a game," Maddie declared.

"Sure we can, we just need a few rules. Rule #1, to start the game, you eat one yellow M&M."

I poured the contents of the bag onto the table and we both grabbed a yellow candy. I popped mine in my mouth right away; Maddie put hers off to her right, for later.

"Hey, you have to eat it, otherwise we can't start the game."

"Oh, okay," she said and a loud crunch turned into a broad, sweeping smile.

I put the M&M's back into the bag. "OK, now we begin. I will dump out one and you guess what color it will be. If you're right, you get to eat it."

"What if I get it wrong?" Maddie asked.

"It goes back in the bag and you guess again."

"You won't eat it?"

"I'm not sure, I really like M&M's," I teased.

"Uncle John, pleeeaase?" she begged, cocking her head to one side and batting her eyes.

"OK, they are all yours." I shook the bag and said, "Go ahead, guess!"

"Purple," Maddie said, starting, of course, with her favorite color.

A blue M&M rolled across the table. She looked up, eyes pleading for the treat.

"There are no purple M&M's," I told her. "Let's see what colors you should guess." Again I poured the bag out.

"Brown, blue, green, yellow, red, orange. A lot of yellows. Keep that in mind, it's important," I added.

"Why?" Maddie asked.

I didn't want to explain probability for the rest of the hour so I just said, "Guess yellow and you should win more."

"OK!"

I shook the bag and Maddie hollered, "Yellow!" Two M&M's fell from the bag, a green and a yellow.

"Whoa, a bonus! Know what that means?"

"No," she said. "What?"

"You get to eat both!" I shouted in my best game show voice.

My Maddie gobbled up the candies and the game continued. After guessing yellow the first ten times I persuaded her to try another color. Soon we changed the game to guessing which hand the M&M was in. When the final M&M was retrieved from the very bottom corner of the bag I placed it in Maddie's right hand. I told her, "OK, if I guess it I get to eat it, if I get it wrong you eat it."

I waited for her to put it behind her back then bring it back out front. She had not yet caught on to switching the M&M when it was out of sight, so I guessed the left hand, and shrieked when she opened her empty palm. "No, no! Please I love M&M's! Just one! you got all the others! It's the last one!"

"Uncle Joohhnnn," she teased with a wicked smile and held the candy over her open mouth.

"No, no, please!"

The M&M disappeared into her mouth, gone with a deafening crunch.

"No!" I roared, and flopped to the ground clutching my chest.

Maddie jumped from the table and piled on top of me, taunting me with her open mouth and tongue covered in the remains of the last M&M, flecks of red shell mixed with melting chocolate. Her laughter rose as my crocodile tears fell. I pounded the ground, weeping face in the dirt.

"No! Not the last one! They're gone, all gone, all gone!"

In the middle of my tantrum Elizabeth appeared at the playground gate. Maddie ran to her and I sat up smiling. I had kept her busy for a whole hour with just a 99¢ bag of M&M's.

*   *   *

On a dreary Sunday, the kind you seldom see in Southern California, early in the winter quarter before things got busy with classes, I went to the supermarket to buy a small cake for Elizabeth's birthday. It was just after the holidays, at the start of the football playoffs, and each aisle was awash in every type of libation imaginable. I sauntered through the store without even a thought of having a drink. It wasn't until I reached the checkout counter, and looked back, that I realized I had just walked through a virtual ocean of alcohol with no desire to have a drink, the absence of this urge documenting a true miracle.

You see miracles can be very small things, they do not always involve the parting of seas. Often they are answers to questions we didn't even know we were asking, or the absence of things we swore we could not be without. They are the kindnesses of strangers, our perseverance during difficult times, our unanswered prayers.

In mid-2011, another miracle occurred. I received a certified letter from the City of San Francisco informing me that I needed to appear in court regarding the expunging of all the legal charges I had accumulated during my time there.

Several months earlier, I had approached attorneys from the *Clean Slate Program* to clear up my criminal record. After gathering character references from my family and Doug, writing a lengthy letter to the judge, and providing transcripts from school, my petition for expunging all charges was granted. After speaking with the lawyers from Clean Slate, I was assured that it was all approved and that the official paperwork would be arriving in a few weeks. I breathed a sigh of relief, secure in the knowledge that the sins of my past would have no bearing on the licenses I would need as an engineer.

Now they were asking me to return to court? I was sure something must have gone wrong. Calls to the office in San Francisco proved fruitless as the answer I got was always the same. "Yes, the judge wants to see you," and, "No, we don't know why."

My head swam with possible reasons for requiring me to appear in person. Perhaps they had unearthed some forgotten warrant or charge I had never faced? My mind raced with possible consequences for something I had done wrong, even though, for the life of me, I had no idea what it could be. I finally concluded that obsessing over something I didn't have a clue even existed a few days before, was not just counterproductive but plain stupid, so I booked a flight to San Francisco to accept whatever punishment awaited.

Arriving in the Bay Area I spent the day before my court appearance relaxing with Doug and Mike in Half Moon Bay. At 6:00 a.m. I borrowed Doug's truck and headed to the court building. The procedures were very familiar, but for the first time I entered the lobby with no fear and headed to Dept. 18, and my designated courtroom.

I met my attorney outside the courtroom doors. I had never met her before, had no knowledge of how she was involved in my case, but I had to ask, "Do you have any idea why I have to be here today? I thought this was a done deal?" I whispered in the hallway.

"No. Let's just wait and see what the judge has to say."

After sitting through a half-dozen cases, most of which ended with smiling petitioners leaving with clean records, I was called forward and stepped to the podium in front of the judge. "Thank you for coming," he began. "I just wanted to meet the man who saw a sign on a bus and turned his life around."

I stood speechless. The only reason I was there was my letter to the judge mentioning the bus placard responsible for my first step towards a degree. Essentially, I had become a kind of poster child for rehabilitation, and by extension, the good accomplished by the San Francisco Department of Corrections. I could not have cared less about all that -- not only did they expunge my record, but they reduced all my cases, including two felony charges, to misdemeanors, and then dismissed them all. I was finally, completely, free of this huge chunk of wreckage from my past. I said, "Thank you," to the judge and my public defender, and drove back to Doug's and my evening flight back to LAX.

*   *   *

The War Wagon

At the end of fall semester 2010, in the middle of my sophomore year, I had been toying with the idea of upgrading my living quarters for some time. I was growing weary of climbing in and out of the bed above my cab, the camper was old, and despite my best efforts, falling apart.

My disability case, now over four years old, seemed to be picking up speed as the lawyers had predicted. It looked like it would be settled before Year 5. I think the strategy of the Social Security Administration is to delay each case at least that long, in the hopes that it will just go away. This is more common than not, as claimants don't respond to the required updates sent out sporadically as the request is processed. Many claimants lose interest, miss an update, and have to start over or even die, all of which leads to uncollected benefits remaining in government coffers.

Because I was in school, and constantly pestering my lawyer, I stayed on top of things and my case was processed as quickly as possible. In early February, I drove to Orange County for my one and only hearing, and was issued a check for $10,000 for the year and a half I was unable to work.

Half the money went to pay off the loan on my pickup, and I planned on leaving the rest in the bank to avoid being dead broke for the rest of my academic career, but that soon changed. Coming down the steep hill from East Shore RV, I braked hard and the camper broke loose and slammed into the cab of the truck. The back window frame popped out of the body without shattering the glass. Inspection of the anchor bolts showed that the wooden frame had simply cracked in two, and the bolts had pulled free, allowing the camper to slide forward. Aside from the popped out window, and the strain on my heart caused by all the racket, the damage inflicted by the camper was minimal, but the warning was clear -- the camper would have to go.

I began scouring Craigslist and Truck Trader for a suitable replacement. Any one of a dozen vehicles could have done the trick -- a small RV, a van, another slide-in camper for the pickup, but I had an idea I was confident would work better than all the rest.

From residing in campers for four years now, I knew many of the tricks of the trade for making life on road, but off of the street, easier. Two items were absolutely necessary: electricity and plumbing. These two facts gave me the basics for creating my own RV, customized to fit my lifestyle and needs.

I needed a reliable platform on which to build the camper, something roomy and cheap, something easy to convert into a home on wheels. I decided on a 1977 Ford Step Van, the same type used by FedEx, UPS, or Frito Lay to make their deliveries, roughly 14' by 7' inside, with a roll-up back door, and began building the War Wagon.

My first challenge was to provide power for the truck. I wanted to be able to stay on campus without worrying about charging batteries. During the summer of 2009, I had added two 120-watt Schott solar panels and a charge controller to the slide-in. The system wasn't adequate to provide all the power I wanted, so I added two more 200-watt Canadian Solar panels, a Morningstar MPPT controller, and six 6-volt golf cart batteries coupled to a 2500 watt modified sine wave inverter to the Wagon. The panels' yield was 4500 watts per day. Matching that with a total storage capacity of 7,920 watts limited to 50% discharge, left me with roughly four kilowatts of useable power per day. I researched different components for the better part of a month before purchasing and assembling the system. My hard work has been rewarded by a flawless performance over the past four years. During peak sunlight hours I can even run my air conditioner to keep the daytime temperature inside the truck down.

I added Polk Audio speakers to a Kenwood stereo, DIRECTV programming an LG LED TV and an internet hotspot to finish off the electrical and entertainment systems.

Plumbing came in the form of the water tank and sink salvaged from the slide-in camper and a porta-potti, leaving showering for the gym or wherever I happened to be staying. I added an electric water pump and faucet to eliminate the hand pump, making washing dishes a whole lot easier.

The final version of the truck was a combination of my sketched, various cabinets, windows, and appliances scavenged from the old slide-in, a pair of damaged cabinets I purchased from Home Depot for $100.00, floor coverings and carpet for the walls that were on sale at Lowes, and lots of insulation to keep the cabin quiet and comfortable.

Construction took a total of two months. I took a page out of my Shelter Network days and dismantled the camper in a weekend, moving the needed parts into the cavernous Step Van. I completed the bulk of the work with a set of Porter Cable cordless tools. I only needed to procure an electrical outlet for my router when applying the Formica tops to some of the countertops I fabricated. I found one in the school's southwest parking lot, on the bottom of a utility panel alongside the track, close enough to the parking lot to allow me to run an extension cord out to the truck.

I slept in the back of the rig as I pieced my home together around me. The first night I spent on my mattress atop the pile of lumber and insulation I was using to finish the inside, a roll of vinyl flooring propped against the wall, with cardboard boxes and cabinets stacked so high in the front of the truck, I could not see out the windshield. The desire to make some type of order out of this chaos kept me working on the truck during every free moment I had that quarter.

The results, were better than I could ever have anticipated. At 22' 6" the truck measures six inches under the 23' legal maximum for on-street parking. I left the roll-up door operational to allow for cool night breezes to flow through and to access my tools stored the bed.

The War Wagon has been a rousing success. It gets about 10 miles a gallon and has served as my home since March 2011. I loaned the pickup to my cousin who was in need of a car, as I wasn't ready to sell the truck, and keeping two vehicles at school would have been pressing my luck.

My crowning achievement was getting the War Wagon reclassified as a motorized home with the DMV and the California Highway Patrol, lowering the registration fees to $90 a year. The current insurance is $140 a year, bringing the annual operating costs to $230 a year, plus gas and oil.

*   *   *

Spring 2011

Between working on the War Wagon, studying for classes and going to the gym, my schedule was pretty full coming into the summer before my senior year. My degree progress hit an unexpected snag during Spring Quarter 2011, which was quickly remedied by my friend, and mentor, Professor Howard Turner.

Senior Project Symposium is a group presentation given by students to industry professionals. It's required for graduation, and can create a real sticking point as students scramble for spots in the competing projects. Professor Turner approached me early in the Spring quarter with his idea for a project. While waiting in the Geospatial lab for class to begin, he barked, "McHugh," from the front of the room in his rough, Northern English accent. I walked to the front of the empty room. "What would you think doing of a 3D scan of the campus?"

I had done several projects for the school before, including mapping the emergency phones and tying them to the computers in the police station to show where calls originated from when they were placed. "Yeah I could do that. Might be kind of fun."

"Would make a nice senior project too."

At lunch the next day I told Steve my good news. "Are you going to do it?" he asked, adding, "'Cause I could use a spot too."

"Let's go talk to Professor Turner and see what we can come up with."

Since Professor Turner was asking me to head the project, it was pretty clear that I would be allowed to participate. Steve, on the other hand, needed an angle to plead his case, and the gleam in the professor's eye told me he already had that covered. "So you're military?" he asked Steve.

"Yes, Sir," Steve answered in true military fashion.

"Well, why would we need a military man on the project?" he mused.

Steve and I looked at each other for an answer. None was forthcoming.

"April 30, 1980, in London the DRFLA (Democratic Revolutionary Front for the Liberation of Arabistan) terrorist group took control of the Iranian Embassy with 26 hostages inside. Six days later they executed the Chief Press Officer and threw the body out into the street." Professor Turner's account provided a history lesson for Steve who was not yet born when the siege occurred, and a reminder of the past for me as I vaguely remember the incident from my early twenties. "The SAS stormed the building and saved all the remaining hostages. We provided the models for the assault."

The lecture was beginning to make sense. "So you guys created mock ups of the building for the attack."

"Right. We used building plans and pictures of the room from press photos to make a walk through for the SAS guys to plan their moves. We could do the same with the 3D scans," Professor Turner said.

"We can use the models for a hostage situation?" asked Steve.

"Hostage, gunman, terrorists, fire. Anything that requires responders to enter a building they don't know," confirmed Dr. Turner.

"Sounds good," I said. With a terse nod, Steve agreed.

"It's settled then," boomed a smiling Professor Turner. "Let's go talk to Netter."

"Netter," actually Professor Neto, was my adviser, as well as the Dean of the department. It would mean clambering to get my prerequisites done, but it paved the way for definitely graduating the following Spring.

The three of us met with Dr. Neto. After describing the idea for a new senior project, and Professor Turner explaining the possibility of securing additional funding for the university, she quietly mulled over the situation. "The problem is that you two are technically not eligible to start Senior Project until after you finish the prerequisites," Dr. Neto began. "I don't know if I can allow it. Quite a few others have asked for the same thing and I told them no."

"But McHugh is the one I want to head this thing, and Steve certainly has paid his dues," countered Professor Turner.

Still, she remained on the fence. I used the lull in the conversation to play my last ace. "Dr. Neto, as Professor Turner pointed out, Steve has served in combat and would be the best student, no scratch that, he would be the only student, who could add to the threat response portion of the project. Me, well I just turned 50, and I'm not getting any younger. I'd kind of like to wrap this thing up while my parents are still alive to see it."

It was the only time I played the age card, but to remain silent would have added another year to my quest to graduate.

"Alright," she answered. "But you have to get Fluid Mechanics finished this summer, then you can start Senior Project in the Fall."

Thus our senior project was born.

First came Fluid Mechanics and Geotechnical Engineering both prerequisites for the Senior Project. Taking summer classes required me to pay full, non-resident tuition. For the two classes ,the bill came to about

291

$5,000, added to the fact that my ability to earn any money during the summer was severely curtailed, and the cost rose to something like $15,000.

Fluids was a challenging course, but a passing grade was all that was required for graduation -- I didn't need to get the normal C or C- to continue with the program. Dr. Maryam Shafahi, an associate professor in the Mechanical Engineering department, taught the Fluids course, an attractive woman with a reputation as a demanding instructor.

Ninety percent of our grade depended on the results of just two exams -- a midterm worth 40%, a final worth 50%, and the remaining 10% attributed to homework and class participation.

I worked hard in the class and felt like I had a good understanding of the complex material. I went to class every day, and did all the homework on my own, working diligently through each problem without consulting a solutions manual. A single problem required a few pages of calculations and might take two hours for someone as inexperienced as me. Our first exam came about four weeks in and I was confident I would pass. The test consisted of two of questions. I solved the first one using a method that was not applicable to the problem, and as a result lost all the credit for my answer. My final grade was a 17 out of 100 -- I was doomed before the class was halfway through.

I wanted to leave. Steve was enrolled in the class as well and I told him. "I don't think this Fluids class is going to work out. There is no way I can pass now, so I might as well start working for the next two months."

"John, just hang in there. At the very least go talk to her," he said, encouraging me to stay.

"I don't know Steve, I just feel like I'm tired of going to school. Taking summer classes was probably a big mistake."

"Maybe, but you're committed now, so at least see what she has to say. Who knows what will happen."

"Alright I will," I acquiesced.

Steve was right about at least one thing, there was a lot at stake -- the money, the time, being admitted to Senior Project and, by extension, graduating the following Spring. I needed to know what my options were and if I could still, somehow, pull this class out.

I am not one to run to the teacher and plead my case for an improved grade. Don't get me wrong, if I add up my scores on a test and the instructor missed a few points, I'm first in line to get my score corrected. When I'm the one who made the mistake, however, I have a hard time justifying asking for a higher score.

I can't say the same for all of my fellow students, some of whom seemed to think that their initial test score was but a starting point for negotiating a final grade. Like Rick Harrison of *Pawn Star,s* they would haggle with the teachers over every point, even when it barely mattered. I can't count the number of times I watched as one of my peers fought for a 95 versus a 93 while I sat quite content with a 78 or some other passing grade.

Dr. Shafahi in her office proved far more approachable than the Dr. Shafahi I had come to know in the classroom. Her pretty smile lulled me into a sense of security that enabled me to open up a little more than I normally would have, and this honesty definitely helped me effectively petition my case for passing the class.

"Dr. Shafahi, you know I understand this material -- certainly better than my test showed."

"I think you do John, but I gave the same test to everyone and I can only go by your grade."

"Well, I don't know what to say. If I use the grading rubric from the syllabus, even if I score 100 on the final, which we both know is not going to happen, I still wouldn't pass the class. I mean, I just spent $3,000 to take this class, now I'm sitting here thinking I should just start working so I at least have something to show for the summer."

"John, I can't change your score, because that would be unfair to the others, but I know you are capable of more than the grade indicates. How about if I give you an extra credit assignment to present to the class? That should raise your grade."

"That's more than fair. Thank you."

"Just keep working hard and you should do fine on the final."

"I just hope it's enough," I mumbled under my breath.

Dr. Shafahi waited until I raised my head to make eye contact. "John, do what I have asked and I promise you won't fail the class."

"Thank you," I said and exited the office.

Steve was happy to hear that I had decided to stay, both for my sake and his, as finishing the class alone would have been brutal. He even asked to be a part of the extra credit assignment since a few extra points wouldn't hurt his average either. An email to Dr. Shafahi confirmed that Steve could participate, as long as the amount of work presented justified his involvement. She was not going to hand out extra points for simply adding Steve's name to the project.

Of course, I was still anxious until she posted our grades. I snuck by with a D, nothing to write home about, but one less course about which I had to worry. As my friend Shannon put it, "You Know what that D means right? Degreee!". To validate my understanding of Fluids, the following quarter, using all the concepts we had learned over the summer, I received an A in Hydraulic Engineering, the follow-up to Fluid Dynamics.

I was truly grateful to Professor Shafahi for her benevolence. Although we didn't become fast friends, I saw her on campus often and always said, "Hello." She returned my greeting with the same genuine "It's nice to see you" expression I had seen that first day in her office. I wanted to tell her to smile more often since she looked really great when she did, but I maintained the decorum suited to addressing a professor.

*   *   *

Fall 2011

Finally senior year the pinnacle of undergraduate education was upon me.

Senior Project was the last major hurdle in my pursuit of a degree. Using point clouds created by a laser scanner we modeled the Engineering building, designed a response plan, and presented the package to Homeland Security to obtain a research grant for the university to continue the process. The remaining spots of the group filled up quickly, with me, Steve, James, Frank, Matt, Jake, Ronnie and Gnouni, our resident software guru. Our team was a spirited bunch who worked hard to a man. We had our moments of doubt and disagreement, but in the end produced a presentation that received rave reviews and an A grade for all. Everyone had really great ideas and there was no shortage of input. My only real task as project manager was to point everyone in the same direction, settle the occasional clash of ideas, and reassure everyone that we were on the right track, and everything was coming out all right.

With a litany of deadlines, due dates and presentations going on Senior year passed in the blink of an eye. Amid all the hoopla of Senior Project, and filling out the requisite applications, and paying the necessary fees to finally graduate, I actually found time to pass my remaining classes and keep my precious GPA above 3.0. I graduated with a 3.06 to be exact.

At 4:00 p.m. on Saturday, June 9, 2012, a typically beautiful Southern California day, I walked with my classmates and friends to the podium at the center of the Cal Poly quad to receive my diploma. Arriving on stage I hugged Dr. Neto so hard I was afraid I crushed her, and my family and friends cheered from the gallery. My mom and dad, and many more made the trip to Pomona to share in my special day, some 30 years overdue. My sister, Julie, was there along with Aunt Betty and Uncle Steve, Aunt Brenda and Uncle Doug, Aunt Josephine, Veronica and the precious Miss Myla, Doug and his brother, Mike, and, my friend Andrea, who always believed in the "better me," the man I strive to become every day. I have never felt as proud as I did that day of anything I have accomplished, and I thank God for guiding me along the path. I gazed at the setting sun from the parking lot where my step van and I slept for nearly eight years, still alive and no longer a homeless bum.

* * *

Epilogue

Inevitably, when people hear my story, they want to know what changed, what made this time different from all the others. I wish I had a simple answer, a set of directions to guide them from the haze and fog of addiction to the clarity of sobriety, the "sunshine of the spirit," but each path is different, and each traveler must find their own way. I offer what worked for me, along with one piece of advice. *Try everything*, from Acupuncture to Zen meditation, and everything in between. Keep what works for you and disregard the rest. It is undeniable that AA works the best for the greatest number of people, so be sure to put that high on your recovery To-Do list. Try, and if you fail, try again. You are doing this not only to save your life, but to create a new life, a life full of wonder, happiness, and fulfillment, along with a sprinkling disappointment, sorrow, and pain, because that is what life is.

Two years have passed since I received my undergraduate degree, and this past June 2014, I earned my Master of Science in Engineering Management. The cast of characters in my life story now includes names like Oladapo, Peyman, Kiana, Paniz, and Matinee. My Facebook page looks like the United Nations roster with many entries in languages I have no understanding of, but I always recognize their smiling faces.

I keep making plans, but life intrudes. My Aunt Betty, so proud of me on graduation day, died suddenly from cancer in September the following year. I was renovating Bill Mazzetti's condo in Lake Tahoe when I got the news she was terminally ill. True friend that he is, he offered to put the project on hold and fly me to Florida to be with my family, but I opted to finish the job and return to help just after the funeral.

Steve reenlisted in the Marines, and I was honored to be present at his commencement ceremony where he was made an officer in the Corps. I still see Tanya and Kelly occasionally in Pasadena, where they both live. My friend Andrea lives in San Francisco, alternately loving and hating me for my refusal to settle down and live a normal life now that I am a "professional."

June proved to be a month of wonder as my son, Sean, married a lovely young woman named April. I was delighted to be a part of the festivities, and was even introduced as Sean's father after their first dance. The reception I got from people I have barely spoken to in years was warm, welcoming, and, to my mind, priceless -- another miracle I had not even considered during my drinking days.

I still sleep in the War Wagon, bouncing around California, working as a contractor to pay my few bills, but soon I'll need to put my brain to work as the years take their toll on my back. My degrees and engineering certification hang firmly on the passenger-side wall, incongruous with the surfer dude vibe the van exudes. These days I don't need much. One of AA's many promises states, "Fear of people and economic insecurity will leave us." My time in the woods enables me to be extremely comfortable and content with the few possessions I have.

Today, my greatest pleasure comes from the relationships I formed in the past, and those I will form tomorrow. For the ability to see and cherish this fact, I am eternally grateful.